Eternity in Our Hearts

[signature] Joshua 24:15

R.C. Sproul Jr.

Eternity in Our Hearts

ESSAYS ON THE GOOD LIFE

DRAUGHT HORSE PRESS
BRISTOL, TENNESSEE

To Laurence Windham

May our adventures take us to eternity,
and across the eighth dimension.

Published by Draught Horse Press, an imprint of Dry Creek Publishing.

P.O. Box 1555, Bristol, Tennessee 37621-1555
877-244-5184 / www.draughthorsepress.com

Cover design and book layout by Kevin McCroskey.

Printed in the United States of America.

Scripture quotations are taken from the New King James Version of the Bible, copyrighted by Thomas Nelson, Inc., 1979, 1980, 1982.

ISBN: 1-4040-0000-3

CONTENTS

FOREWORD

How hard it is to get modern conservative Christians to drink Christ deeply! We so easily spend our lives preparing to be martyrs under some pagan blade that we don't ever really *live* life. Living for the extremes of war leaves vast areas of life uncharted.

And being a martyr is relatively cheap and easy; the choices are usually pretty stark, and the tradition promises glory. Some evangelicals spend their time longing to be snapped away in order to avoid living life, and others think that "redeeming the time" means constantly readjusting scaffoldings of theological sentences. But tinkering with theological ideas doesn't require a back brace. The end is that few of us are really interested in the painfully hard work of daily living.

This delightful collection of passionate yet humble musings from R.C. Sproul, Jr. seeks to embrace daily living head on. So many books about the Christian worldview are so boringly mathematical in their attempt to stack the most general of Christian ideas too neatly. But after decades of such books we should start to long for more specifics, more earth and blood and breath. R.C. Jr. aims to do just that. Instead of being satisfied with just broad ideas, he calls us to live Christ in the small things, the way we speak, recreate, eat, grow, and fight. As he says, "we don't need to manufacture holy moments, for they are all around us."

The theme of these essays, and of the magazine from which they are taken—*Every Thought Captive*—is to "live deliberately." Even the more mature Christians around us tend to fail at this. We absorb so many ugly assumptions from the life-hating paganism around us that they seems normal. Even where you might disagree with his exhortations you will be provoked to do better. As he and the Highland Study Center "enjoin folks to live more deliberate lives, [they] are encouraging them to look deep within themselves, to see those weeds of the world that lurk there in the dark corners, those unspoken and too often unexamined assumptions that have no biblical foundation."

The effect of these essays to a Christian mind should be relief; the temptations which surround us are not so much analyzed into oblivion as simply unveiled for their petty ugliness. A healthy Christian life can't help but spot the boring nature of non-Christian culture, especially those parts that most seek to seduce us with pseudo beauty.

Clearing away debris is the easy part, though, and these essays aim to do more. Their weight rests on building, on constructing a positive life, a deliberate life. And yet in the hands of others, these exhortations could be pedantic and arrogant. God's grace has given R.C. Jr's writing a truly disarming humility. These exhortations reveal someone imperfect like us, someone wrestling with living Christ day by day in ways that our traditions have not fully grappled with yet. Christian reality is so deep and rich that to speak otherwise at this time would be instantly transparent. These essays are kisses on the lips—given, you know, the right lips.

My deepest reservation, and I'll warn you quickly, is that he is far, far too easy on the contemporary scourge of holiness, that tyrannical destroyer of hope—the New York Yankees.

DOUGLAS JONES
Senior editor of that "other" magazine,
Credenda/Agenda

Introduction

I have written books, and I have written magazine articles. Each has its own strengths and weaknesses. When I write a magazine article, in only a matter of weeks I get to see it—my work—right there in print. It often doesn't take too long to write, and it often doesn't take too long to read. Books, on the other hand, take me rather a long time to write, and an inordinate length of time to get into print—if they get into print at all.

Books when they are finished usually meet one of two pleasant ends; once the buyer has read them, they are either passed on to friends (at least I hear that happens to other people's books), or they find a nice stately place to rest on a bookshelf somewhere, waiting for that time when someone else might want to read them. Magazine articles, however, are disposable; when we're done with them we either send them to the landfill or use them to wrap fish. Magazines provide a quick turnaround, but the gain is short-term; books have a turnaround measured in eons, but they can give a lasting return.

But occasionally something wonderful happens. For Ligonier Ministries I edit a magazine called *Tabletalk*, which has no doubt wrapped many a fish. Still, eight different times publishers have graciously decided that the fruit of my labors—keeping in mind that my labors were mostly to edit the writings of men smarter than I am—was worthy of a longer incarnation, and so created books from them. The fish wrapping sometimes graduates to bookshelf dressing.

As the director of the Highlands Study Center I edit another magazine, *Every Thought Captive*, that is far more obscure than *Tabletalk* magazine. The U.S. Post Office probably loses more copies of *Tabletalk* monthly than the total copies we mail of *Every Thought Captive*. We are not inundated with requests from folks wanting their *ETC*. But as with all writers, the pieces I write for *ETC* are my children. I love what we do in *ETC*, even if it hasn't become the latest thing. And in God's grace, again a publisher—this time a novice—has decided that these children ought not fade into fishy-smelling obscurity. What you hold is the result of that fateful error in judgment.

I do have a theory as to why *ETC* is not a topic of conversation around Reformed water coolers the world over. For such a little magazine, *ETC* carries a great deal of freight. We at the Center try to be efficient with the limited space we have. And the Center has a peculiar goal, one we keep before us at all times: to help Christians live more simple, separate, and deliberate lives to the glory of God and for the building of His kingdom.

To work efficiently toward this peculiar goal, we take a peculiar approach: we write without frills. We write straightforwardly, directly, and at times prophetically. We offer challenges to the prevailing wisdom, and we do so recklessly. We make people mad—not generally a part of the formula for growing your mail list. We do this not because we are careless, but because we are care-*ful*. We care that the church of Christ is stained with worldliness. We care that the church has substituted the normal for the biblical. And we care that the church doesn't seem to care.

Our style is as old as the hills. We encourage Christians to be more simple in part by not massaging them with our message. We believe that a simple people can take simple truths, even when they are hard truths. We don't sneak up on people, using a rhetorical bait and switch. We do not disguise, nor do we dodge. We lay our convictions out on the table and ask you to choose.

This is also how we encourage Christians to be more separate. We want our readers to understand more fully the antithesis that is the context of our lives. From the time the serpent spoke the first lie, we Christians have been engaged in a war. We were once the seed of the serpent, doing all that we could—even though we might not have known it—to thwart the kingdom of God. But God, while we were yet rebels, loved us and regenerated us. We who were once children of the dark have been made children of the light. And when we go back to the ways of the world, we become like the Hebrews who were tempted to neglect so great a salvation. We are like the children of Moses, carried to a land flowing with milk and honey as on the wings of eagles, to whom Joshua asked, "Choose ye this day whom you will serve."

Our writing is direct and at times jolting so that it might aid in making that choice—that it might wake us from our lethargy and lead us to be deliberate in all that we do and say. We encourage our readers to consider the habits of their hearts, to reflect on why we do the things we do, to take every thought captive.

What you now hold in your hand has been gleaned from columns I have written for *Every Thought Captive*. The only editing that has been done is correction of typos, rewording of phrases, and removal of direct references to the magazine itself. I want the book to stand on its own. But now that these words have made their way from *ETC* into a more permanent form, I do not want them to become mental wrapping for mental fish. I pray that these essays will serve you as tools, as weapons in our warfare with the world, the flesh and the devil.

I also pray that, as you run these rhetorical gauntlets, you will see the beauty of what we seek to do here at the Center. I pray that you will take what I have written not as a slap in the face but an invitation. I pray you will see that as we proceed to live more simple, separate and deliberate lives, we are not simply sealing ourselves off from the world around us, but living faithfully as citizens of the world to come; we are about the King's business.

As the western world descends into the momentariness of the modern, as it chases after the wind of Vanity Fair, we at the Center want to be a people who have eternity not only in our hearts, but in our minds and in our hands. We want to be a people whose goal is simply this: to fear God and to obey all that He commands, knowing that everything is beautiful in its time.

CHAPTER I

Myth
Became Fact

ℰ

And the Word became flesh and dwelt
among us, and we beheld His glory, the
glory as of the only begotten of the Father,
full of grace and truth.

☙

John 1:14

One holdover from our modernist past is that we think *myth* is synonymous with *false*. We also tend to think that it means *old*. And now in our postmodern maturity we have reached the conclusion that while myth is not true, truth is a myth. But there is an important distinction between a myth and a lie, one that—sadly—Bill Moyers and Joseph Campbell understand better than we do. The good news is that C.S. Lewis understood it as well, and explained the distinction brilliantly in a little essay called "Myth Made Fact." (This essay, by the way, is one of many fine Lewis essays in the collection *God in the Dock*.)

Many have sought to make anti-apologetical hay out of the historical fact that there are all sorts of religions that have, as a part of their story, not only a flood myth but even a dying and rising God. Some have used this fact to argue the Christian message is necessarily borrowed from these older and now nearly forgotten religions. Others have argued that this notion of a dying and rising God, even if it is not borrowed, flows out of some Jungian collective unconscious and therefore cannot be true.

Lewis countered these arguments in an unusual way. He did not claim that the Christian story is so different in its details from the others that these accusations do not stand. He claimed that there is only one important difference between our story and the others—that our story is history, that our myth invaded time and became reality.

Have you ever wondered why one weak-spined, pagan king made his way into our most universal confession? When we recite the Apostle's Creed, we say of Jesus that He "suffered under Pontius Pilate." Did that ever seem strange to you? I believe that statement is there for this very reason: Jesus lived in real space and real time; He suffered under a real man, in a real place. Our faith is indeed ancient, going back to the righteous sacrifice of the first martyr, Abel—but it did not grow up in the misty tradition of a prehistoric people. While the Holy Spirit did come and inspire the New Testament, He did not do it

1800 years later as the Mormons claim, through a prophet seated behind a curtain, using magic glasses to read golden plates.

Lewis went one step further than most apologists. He argued not only that these myths are not evidence *against* the Christian faith, but that they are evidence *for* it. He reasoned that the existence of these myths demonstrates that the message of the cross is built into the very nature of reality. (Please don't get your presuppositional hackles up—he did not argue that the gospel message can be understood and embraced through the myth.)

Lewis also saw a sort of universal pre-evangelism in both the myths and the humdrum realities from which they spring. From the fact that the seed corn must die so the corn might flourish in the fields springs the myth of a great Corn King who sacrifices his son for the good of the crop—but also the truth of a God who sends His Son that His bride might be won. The temporal reality—corn—points to a spiritual non-reality—the Corn King—which in turn points to a temporal and spiritual reality—the historical Jesus, who lived, died, and was resurrected.

This understanding can not only serve us as tool in our apologetical tool shed, it can also empower our imagination. I remember watching the movie *Excalibur*—not for the first time, but for the first time after reading Lewis on myth. (Beware, beware—some scenes are suitable for the fast-forward button.) *Excalibur* was released in the early 80s as an almost comic retelling of the life of King Arthur; not at all a piece of serious art. But for a young man who had never seen the frolic of Broadway's *Camelot* or trudged through *Morte d'Arthur*, it was a great introduction to this wonderful story. I watched Arthur ride off to battle Mordred, he and his remaining knights riding horseback through fields of flowering dogwoods—and remembered the myth of the dogwood, that of such was made the cross on which Christ hung. I watched Arthur drive the spear his enemy had put into his side deeper into himself so that he could slay the devil Mordred—and remembered that Christ sacrificed Himself for us, and crushed the head of the serpent. I watched as Arthur was carried off as by angels to Avalon, with the promise that the once king would also be future king—and understood that this same Jesus would return in like manner. From there I moved backward, seeing the Knights of the Round Table as disciples, and Lancelot either as Judas or as Peter.

And from that point I went to the movies in search of Jesus. I did so not because I believe there is a secret conspiracy of Christian screenwriters in Hollywood, but because I believe it is in Him and through Him and to Him that we live, that this is His world, and He is inescapable. Disney's *Tron*, a sort of eighties version of *The Matrix*, not only told the gospel but told it from a distinctly Reformed perspective—this was so clear, though, I believe it had to be intentional. *E.T.* had so many Christian themes running through it that there is a rumor that Steven Spielberg worried out loud whether in making the film he was being untrue to his Jewish heritage.

And there He is in Oz as well. Some have seen in Baum's fantasy story a repudiation of the Christian faith (as well as a host of other subtle intentions; some say it is a screed against the gold standard.) The great, unsung Sean Connery film *Zardoz* says as much; the savage warrior learns that the warrior god he worships is not real when he discovers a copy of *The Wizard of Oz*. Baum's wizard is not real, but a carnival barker employing a powerful combination of technology and show biz. We learn that all we need is within us, and that the dream of a place over the rainbow, when there's no place like home, is only that—a silly dream.

While this understanding has much to go for it, we cannot be sure; such might have been the author's intention, but Jesus has crashed his party. Dorothy comes to Oz from another world. She has left behind all that was familiar to her. She is assaulted by the forces of darkness, heals the sick, is locked up as for dead, escapes and destroys the evil one—which, you'll remember, she had to do before she could go home. The witch's minions rejoice to have been set free from the dominion of the devil. And Dorothy ascends back to her home. However reluctantly, the little girl from Kansas reminds us of the Man from Galilee. This story teaches us more about the Bible than *The Omega Code*.

Imagination, what some might call "the poetic vision" and what others might call a Hebrew rather than a Greek mindset, is needed to see these things. The muse doesn't come in the context of high-tech gadgetry and cold, abstract reasoning; in fact, nothing kills the muse faster. God is not the author of confusion. But neither is He a mathematician; He is, instead, a poet. This fact need not send us off into New Age fantasies; I am not arguing that the path to spiritual maturity is figuring out the sound of one hand clapping. But an understanding that God is a poet can reveal to us the depth and the beauty of the gospel.

God's poetry, as Lewis points out, is restricted neither to movies nor to myths passed around campfires in ancient worlds. He writes in writing, but He also writes in living. We find as much poetry in the gospel as we find gospel in our poetry—but there is yet more. For He lives His lines through our lives. The flesh enlivens the poetry as the poetry sings the flesh.

Consider the analogy Paul gives us in Ephesians between the work of Christ for His church and the relationship of a husband and wife. Paul is not merely using a universal experience to explain a spiritual reality; he is not giving us a mere word picture to help us understand more words. This is in fact how God designed marriage. The relationship between the two is not synthetic but analytic. Or, to put it more poetically, the two images—Christ and the church, husband and wife—are one flesh. Jesus is the Word, the Myth made flesh. And marriage is the Flesh made flesh once more, by design.

But I raise that analogy only by way of analogy, for this is true of all of our lives. As we care for the sick we are Christ to them, just as they are Christ to us. As we coax eggs from chickens, He exercises His dominion over us, just as we exercise dominion over the chickens. As we suffer we are a flesh and blood picture of the Suffering Servant. This is why we are here: to make visible—enfleshed—the glory of God. This is our reason for being.

For too many the Christian life is a myth, in the sense that it is false. They believe that we cannot live all our lives to the glory of God. They believe that we cannot love our neighbor as we love ourselves. They believe that we cannot love our wives as Christ loves the church. And so they grab as reality the ways of the world, and embrace the myth that they will still one day make it over the rainbow.

My desire in this work is to offer not the mere propositions of the faith—though those are vitally important, as it was the Word that was made flesh—but also a guide to living the faith in space and time. I want us, despite our multitude of warts and sins, to make the myth flesh.

In this book I write personally and directly, but not as a stunt. I use directness not as a crass method of standing out in the crowd, but as a reminder to the reader that there is a real person behind these ideas—a person who happens to be rather direct. I tell myself over and over again, "Just say it like you were talking to someone, because that's all you are doing." And all of us—my family and my community—live in real space and real time, where babies are born, where snowmen are built, where teeth are lost, and where—alas—chickens die a futile death.

What you are reading are the thoughts of one man. But my hope is that just as these thoughts have been born in our lives, just as they are the myths that have come from the flesh, so too will they bear much fruit in your lives. My prayer is that we will spend time together, learning from each other how to live this myth. And that in doing so we will go far in living the myth. My fear is that you will read this as just a set of interesting propositions, sometimes poetically phrased; and, like the temporarily curious men who heard Paul at Mars Hill, you will move on as soon as something newer and more interesting comes along.

As you read, I hope you'll see Oz in dazzling Technicolor. I hope that your eyes will grow wide, and you will exclaim with joy, "We're not in Kansas anymore, Toto!"—and then realize that we never were.

Neil Postman's *Amusing Ourselves to Death* is one of those books that changed my life. I'm not given to being rather free with superlatives; I'm stingy with them—but not when it comes to this book.

The first terrific thing about the book is its title. We have a tendency to think of amusement as synonymous with entertainment. We might better think of it in a more sinister way. Those who "muse" think, and think carefully. The prefix *a-* means *not* or *non*. An *a*-theist is one that says there is no god. A person who is *a*-moral has no morals. Perhaps, then, when we are *a*-mused, we are not thinking.

We often speak about the idiot box this way. After a long and tiring day we just want to sit and look, to "veg out". We don't want to think—and our friends in Hollywood are happy to oblige. We stop thinking for a few hours and take a mental nap, the kind you can be awake enough to enjoy.

The book begins with a powerful analogy that has on more than one occasion made its way into my own writing. He notes that while conservatives have manned the ramparts against tyranny, standing against Orwell's vision of *1984*, too few of us have sounded the alarm about a less well-known but more chilling dystopian future, the one laid out by Aldous Huxley in *Brave New World*. Orwell, you'll remember, gave us the terror of Big Brother, that all-seeing totalitarian monster. But Huxley gave us the more benign vision of a populace lulled into a complacent slumber through the twin evils of perpetual amusement and *soma*, a euphoric, sleep-inducing drug. Like the poppies placed by the Wicked Witch as Dorothy and her companions had almost reached their goal of Oz, *soma* calls the people to sleep, to forget, to rest; *soma* calls the people to a black sabbath.

Postman argues that television is our *soma*, that it has lulled us to sleep. And as with all the devil's ploys, television not only carries a deadly downside but it doesn't even provide the thing promised. Not only do you lose your soul, but you don't ever really get what you bargained for, either. The television may give a rest to our bodies and minds, but it agitates our souls. The constant shifting of the camera angle, the incessant flow of disjointed images give no rest. To be sure, our guard is down; since television is image-based and not proposition-based, our rational faculties are not engaged, . But those images stick with us and, as we sleep, turn themselves into propositions straight from the source—the father of lies.

Postman does not argue that such is the result of some sort of conspiracy. He points out that the overlords of Hollywood are interested in just two things: they want to make a lot of money, and they want us to think like they do. They are not self-consciously trying to put us to sleep. But for all his wisdom Postman is not a believer, and so his worldview does not allow for conspiracies so well buried that they reach into the very pit of hell. He is right that the moguls do not know what they are doing. But the serpent who pulls their strings knows exactly what he is doing.

What makes the Huxleyan view more chilling than the Orwellian view is perhaps this: we do not need to be cowed to be put to sleep; instead we ask for our dose, and take it happily. Big Brother does not threaten that he is watching us, but we watch him—because we want to. And as with *soma*, we need a stronger and stronger dose each time to get the same non-rush, whether that dose be more time in front of the machine, or more action, or more comedy, or more melodrama while we're there.

But that's also the good news. I've made an amazing discovery in my own journey away from the poppy fields. When you turn off the TV, no flying monkeys come to get you. Big Brother doesn't send the local gendarmes down to teach you a lesson. No jealous bureaucrats tell the King that you're not bowing down to the proper idol and you need a serious sauna. All one has to do is turn it off.

And then came another blessing. Once I got out of the poppy field, I discovered that poppies stink. I didn't want to go back, not because I knew it was wrong or dangerous, but because it wasn't any fun anymore. Professional TV bashers, including Neil Postman and Ken Myers, always shy away from the big application; having decimated the legitimacy of television, they stop short of telling us never to watch. And so we go on the way we were.

Now, I will also stop short of telling you never to watch the television. But I do have a suggestion for judging how much watching is too much: if you find that you want to watch it, then you're still at least half-asleep. You'll know you've cut back enough when you don't want to watch at all. That's a joyous thing, like discovering that ice cream is good for you and zucchini stunts your growth. For what we do with our time should be joyful. Play cards with your family. Read a good book, like Neil Postman's. Write a letter to an author. Try raising chickens—well, don't do that. Start musing, and you just might find it entertaining.

You'll discover, if you can just gut it out until the withdrawal symptoms go away, that better than Central Perk, better than Springfield, better than Providence, there's no place like home.

The grand special effect that caught the eyes of the audience in *The Wizard of Oz* was—color. That's it, just color. And they were dazzled. And though there were some exciting events, the effects were not up to our modern standards. But as the tornado closes in on the family farm one can't help but be concerned and excited. A tornado has three key elements of excitement: speed, power, and unpredictability. I've seen my share of natural disasters: I've lived in Florida and I've experienced hurricanes; I've lived in San Francisco and I've experienced earthquakes; I've lived in Kansas and I've experienced tornadoes. The irony, in the providence of God, is that I also experienced all three of these wild rides while living in Pennsylvania. I'm a weather junkie. There has never yet been a storm that I have not wished to experience, from the center. When the rain, thunder and winds come our way, my wife Denise is doing well if she can keep me in the sunroom of our house; she won't coax me all the way inside, though—I want to be in the middle of it.

Perhaps the appeal is that it seems like such a safe danger, that it gives thrills without guilt. God, I think, isn't going to get angry with me. I'm endangering no one else, and I'm not breaking His law. But those considerations did not always stop me in my own pursuit of excitement. Not only have I experienced some serious weather, so too have I experienced some serious sin. I've lost my lunch a time or two from overindulging in the fruit of the vine. I've been pursued by the law; once for entering where I should not have—I was exploring an abandoned hospital—and once for not allowing others to enter where they should not have—I was blocking the doors of an abortion mill. I could go on cataloguing the sins of my youth, but the point is that when I was young I did many things I shouldn't have.

Could my youth have been any different? Of course not. Did God use my sins for my good and His glory? Absolutely. Do I want my children to go through the same things? Not on your life. I want to shelter my children, and I say so without apology. I no more want my children to walk through the storm of youthful rebellion than I want them playing outside when the funnel cloud comes blowing through. I want them in the cellar where they belong, where it is safe.

Some argue against homeschooling on the grounds that such is sheltering children. I always reply, "What are you going to accuse us of next—feeding and clothing our children?" This parenting philosophy, that we must throw our lambs to the wolves so that they might become brave, is thinly veiled folly.

The argument is so transparent that I wonder that those who make it aren't ashamed of their nakedness. They are saying this: it is work to guard the hearts of our children; it is no easy thing to fend off those who would consume them. I mean, how are we supposed to watch *NYPD Blue* if we won't let the kids watch it? It seems far better to order the sheep to watch over themselves than to stop running with the wolves. They abdicate their responsibilities, and call it courage, or wisdom.

Children need to be sheltered, to be protected. They need to be protected from themselves, and from those who would lead them astray. They are not ready to reason out the will of God in all circumstances; far less are they ready to defeat temptation in whatever form it comes. While God certainly can and does use sin for good, just as He can use a storm, we cannot sin that providential grace might abound all the more.

My children, like all children, are sinners; they were born that way. But that doesn't mean they need to become experts on sin. Wise, yes—jaded, no. While they are by no means innocent before the throne of God in themselves, I still want to maintain their 'innocence' as long as possible. They don't need to know about crack houses, child-beaters, homosexuals and pornography. And lacking that knowledge doesn't make them ignorant, either. They do know about spouses who failed to keep their promises. They know that some children disobey all the time, and that some mommies and daddies disobey God by not punishing their disobedient children. They do know about death. They do know that some mommies kill their babies, that many people worship false gods, and that often those who love Jesus are sent to prison or killed. In short, they know the Bible, and what it teaches—that the world is full of sin, as are we.

I shelter my children. I would sooner have my children left out in a tornado than placed in the hands of a professional priest of the religion of the state, a government school teacher. When are they ready to go out and win the lost for Jesus? Here's a good rule of thumb. Winning souls, and protecting your own soul, is far more difficult and more important than making a living. If they can't do the latter, don't send them out to do the former. If you wouldn't send them out to fight a grown teacher with their fists, why expect them to do it with their wits, especially when the teacher has the whole world cheering him on?

Shelter is good, and not something which we should be ashamed of providing to our children. There are things children don't need to know, and keeping them from that knowledge is service to the King. If your children think that *gay* means *happy* and *queer* means *odd* , you are doing a good thing. Stand firm against the wolves who growl at you that you are sheltering your children. Tell them what one little girl learned the hard way—there's no place like home.

Chapter

Home, Sweet Home

❧

*In My Father's house are
many mansions; if it were not so,
I would have told you.
I go to prepare a place for you.*

☙

John 14:2

When the self-help gurus are trying to coax us into the up-by-the-bootstraps position, they often throw out this little nugget of wisdom: "Any job worth doing is worth doing well." Being the trained professional slacker that I am, I have managed to turn this motivational goad inside out. (I am a professional—please do not try this at home.) If any job worth doing is worth doing well, doesn't it follow that any job you cannot do well isn't worth doing? It is my practice to sooth my conscience for my perennial weaknesses by denigrating the importance of those things I cannot seem to do. Keeping one's work area neat—that's something for small minds to do. Getting chickens to lay eggs—that's a matter of complete indifference in the grand scheme of things. This little twist works wonders for my self-image, and we all know how important *that* is.

The trouble is that sometimes I have trouble doing things I'm supposed to be able to do well. I am, while wearing several of my hats, a professional wordsmith. You will never catch me saying, "You know, it doesn't really matter if I can't communicate very well. What difference could that make?" I spend far too much time teaching either with my pen or my tongue to lose interest in words. Yet, try as I might—and after having five years now to learn how—I still haven't succeeded in communicating what it is that we do here at the Highlands Study Center, nor what it is that we love so deeply about it. Words fail me—or, rather, I fail words.

There are some things I *am* able explain about what we do. You all know what a magazine is; we publish one called *Every Thought Captive*. All of you can grasp what a Bible study is, like the ones we offer on Tuesday and Thursday evenings. All of you have had classes before, and so you have some idea of what we provide to homeschooled children at the Highlands Academy. And I venture to guess that nearly all of you have been to a conference or attended camp at some point in your lives, and so you can imagine what happens at our conferences and at the annual Summer Camp for Couples. But as much as we enjoy doing them, these 'programs' are not really what we do. And they certainly are not what we are.

Another approach I could take would be to run through a list of the things we're for. We're covenantal, agrarian—or at least want to be—and Reformed. We believe in homeschooling, courtship, and headship. We leave our family size in the hands of God, and we lead His resultant blessings into worship daily. We make our own salsa, our own bread, some of our daughters' dresses, and our own beer. In short, we're a hardy band of prairie muffins, although of the Scottish variety. But that's not it either.

What we are escapes words, not because the words are not powerful enough, but because they are *too* powerful. When we take the poetry of the grace of God and try to restate it as some sort of equation, when we try to crunch the numbers of God, something amorphous, ethereal—something that is at once full of power and impossible to pinpoint—slips through our fingers like quicksilver. What we're left with is nuts and bolts, even perhaps a schematic drawing—but the life has left. The best word I can come up with is 'home'.

What we love about our little community is that there is a *here* here. Where we are is distinct from everywhere else. Some of those elsewheres are also distinct, but such places are fewer and fewer. Too many places are turning into indistinguishable collections of strip malls filled with indistinguishable exercise clubs, Hallmark stores and Blockbuster Video stores, with an Arby's somewhere out front in the parking lot. In these towns you can drive a few blocks for a change of pace—to find a strip mall with a K-Mart, a hair salon and a bad Chinese restaurant. And if you're in the city you can drive a few miles up the interstate to the next suburb and see the same thing all over again.

Here in southwest Virginia we have mountains that are molehills next to the Rockies and forests that are so much grass next to the redwoods of California. We have a river running through it that is a brook next to the Mississippi. God has not blessed us with overwhelming superlatives—but He has given us a place.

Home, however, is not just about geography. We know we are home when we see the same old diner that has long been feeding generations. But we also know we are home when we see the same old folks in that diner. That we stay and make it home helps to make it home.

The center of this is, of course, our Reformed community. On every Sunday evening that is the fifth Sunday of the month, we worship together with five other area Reformed circles. No church is there trolling for new members; no church is there to pick a fight over liturgical versus traditional worship, or over classical versus presuppositional apologetics. We're there to see our friends.

Recently two of those friends hosted a baby shower for a third friend, Monique Dewey, who was about to give birth to her seventh child. She and Mark, and the children as their family has grown, had traveled all over the country before settling here. Mark's work had taken him to Michigan, Louisiana, California, New York, Florida and Pennsylvania. And Monique had given birth to her first six children with not a single shower being held in her honor. There's something wrong with that; if we cannot join in with friends to celebrate the impending arrival of a new blessing, we're far from home.

But it doesn't stop there. My attempt to describe home, to reduce the reality of home to something that can be expressed in words, somehow takes something out of the real thing. In the same way, the creation of fellowship programs in the church robs us of some of the joy and meaning of the fellowship. Scheduling fellowship is not unlike scheduling time for bouncing baby on the knee; the charm evaporates for both parties.

We run into our friends in part because we do not live in a megapolis. Our circles are small enough, and we live close enough to one another, that our paths cross even when we don't plan for it. We run into each other at the grocer and at the diner. We pass each other on the road, and no matter how many more miles we have to go, we know that we are home.

Though time spent together is sweetest when it is spent with like-minded people, we find ourselves rejoicing even when we run into those with whom our ideological kinship is not so tight. I visit with my local homebrew supplier Frank when I am in his shop, and I see him when we are both in the veterinarian's office. I ask after Myra, his chronically overweight Labrador, and he asks after my children—all of whom love to go to Frank's and visit Myra. We run into our dentist at the county fair and at the piano teacher's house.

The result is not flashy. I don't get an overpowering home 'high' when these things happen. But that's not what home is about. Home is sweet, not spicy. This sense of place gives a sense of peace. It is more an anchor than a big wave to surf, more the strong tower than the bungee ride down.

We have this sense of place because we have sought it. For many of the locals a sense of place is as natural—and as unnoticed—as the air they breathe. We came here, however, because there was no air to breathe in the many places we came from.

We were deliberate in choosing this simplicity, and that sets us apart, makes us separate. We don't have access to the beach, nor to multi-mile long ski runs. We do not have high-speed cable access to the internet, but we are quite at home on this side of the digital divide. We don't even have a Thai restaurant within an hour's drive. What we have is a home, a place where even though we don't yet talk like the locals, we know we belong.

And while I can hope against hope that my children will catch the accent, I can be assured that they will grow up to be like the locals, not even knowing that it is possible to not be home. I know that they will never know that the world is filled with sad and wandering wretches who left home in search of a pot of gold on the other side of the rainbow.

Our children will forget when we arrived, and like a child in a dream, even as they grow older they will believe that they have always been here. This place will be to them as the water is to the fish, as it has become to us, a source of daily life. And so they will certainly fail to thank us. But their peace, their sense of place, will be all the thanks we need.

This is not really a sales pitch—or, rather, it is not an attempt to persuade you to move here. But it *is* a sales pitch for you to make a home somewhere. Get close to God's covenant people. Get to know your neighbors, and those with whom you transact business. Be a neighbor, as Christ has commanded. Get out of the rat race. Find a sense of place, and when you have, you will know that you must never leave. For you will have found your own little corner of heaven, one that will be joined with ours and all similar corners of the world in the eternal heavens and the eternal earth. Put your heart where your home is, and you will never be sorry. Fail to do so, and you will never go home.

We all know that there is more to a home than a house, that a home is more than just a place to hang your hat. But we are less sure of what that added dimension might be. It is a mystery, like that cake we already ate, that eludes us. As one who too often must hang my hat in the impersonal confines of the standard American motel, I can tell you the difference between house and home does not lie in physical comfort. In the motel I have better reception on the television and many more channels. I have more room in my bed and a tidier desk to work on. I have private control of the room temperature and never find stockings drying in the shower. There are no lingering reminders of dirty diapers and no Kix crumbs sticking to the bottoms of my feet.

What makes a house a home is not that the house is bigger than the motel room, but that the home is bigger than *me*. Home is the place where I fit in. It is that place where I am joined with something much bigger than myself. (And keep in mind that I'm so fat that when I sit around the house, I sit *around* the house.) In a house I am isolated, cut off, alone, no matter how many people might share the same roof; in a home

I am never alone, even when there is no one else there. A home is a place of comfort because it is a collective.

We are torn in two directions on this whole matter of identity. You see it illustrated best among the disaffected youth who don the shock wear of the day. Whether it is green spiked hair, or the pancake make-up and black nails favored by the Goth gaggle, young people always take that heroic stand for individualism with all their like-thinking, like-dressing friends, all based on the mass-produced angry music and angry literature that distinguishes this crowd. They are the misunderstood loners, this massive crowd of cookie-cutter individualists.

We who have reached the age at which we have no hair to spike feel something of the same pull, though we usually express it in less dramatic ways. We want to be the lone hero; we want to determine our own identity. We wouldn't think of succumbing to group-think—everybody knows how horrible *that* is.

The reality is that we do need—and rightly have—an identity larger than ourselves. That identity is broadest not as citizens of the planet, as our would-be U.N. masters would have us think. It is not as good Americans, nor even as sons of the south; it is broadest in the kingdom of heaven, where we are one with all God's people, even the ones that irritate us. The circle within that circle is the local expression of the catholic church. And the circle within *that* circle is the family. What makes a house a home is that we are one thing together, just as what makes a church building a church is that we are one thing together with all who profess the true faith.

But there are faux homes invading our houses, alternate identities that seek to seduce us. We receive a counterfeit comfort when our identity is more with the guys down at the bar, or the girls down at wherever girls go when they go out together. More important, our children are susceptible to these fake families. We panic when our girls find their corporate identity in an undying love for the shy one of the Back Street Boys or an unquenchable dream to be just like that Spears girl. The problem, however, is not merely that morality is absent in the crowds our children identify with, but that the identity they seek is outside the home. It will not be a great leap forward if our daughters see girls who own American Girl dolls as their family.

While mooning over a Back Street Boy (or even a rock star with talent) and gyrating in front of a mirror like Britney are things I hope I'll never see my daughters do, and while I'm perfectly content for them to play with their American Girl dolls, I want them to know that they belong to *our* family, that this is *our* home. I want them to know that they are defined first by this covenant we are in together with our brothers and sisters around the world; and second, by the fact that we are Sprouls. There is content within that name that goes far beyond the address of our home; there is a history of shared experiences and shared convictions. They know this, but only because my wife and I are careful to tell them.

We are all on a quest together—to grow in obedience, to become more godly, to make manifest the reign of the King who redeemed us. In addition, we say *dinner* instead of *lunch*, and *supper* instead of *dinner*. We root for the Pittsburgh Steelers. We love Mommy's bread and her granola, and we laugh that daddy tends to burn the grilled cheese sandwiches. We rejoice when the chickens produce, and more often we share a dose of stoicism when they don't.

What feeds this family identity that makes our house a home is that we *live* within it. We actually act like a family, because we try to do things as a family. We all watch Andy Griffith together. We all participate in family and corporate worship together. We go to the lake together and visit our friends together. We go to school together and we even go to Bible study together. We play games together. We even—gasp!—eat our meals together. We are always home wherever we are, if we are together, because our family *is* our home.

It is not kitsch from some country knick-knack store that makes a house a home. It is not a white picket fence, or a cuddly dog. It is not the smell of fresh-baked cookies—in fact, such is sufficient to create intense moments of every-man-for-himself individualism. It is simply the shared conviction that we share convictions and loyalties, hardships and joys. It is our unity in affirming and enjoying our unity.

❧

They say it goes back to the English Common Law, but I believe it goes back much further—all the way back to the garden. It is a legal principle that ought to be so obvious that it need not be stated. Were it not for an intrusive, invasive, insatiable, insidious institution known as the state, it would not need to be stated. The English expressed it poetically: every man's home is his castle. Our forefathers, leaning less on the familial side and more on the legal side of covenants, said it this way: "The right of the people to be secure in their persons, houses, papers, and effects, against unreasonable searches and seizures, shall not be violated, and no Warrants shall issue, but upon probable cause, supported by Oath or affirmation, and particularly describing the place to be searched, and the persons or things to be seized." Do you recognize that phrase? It is the fourth amendment to the Constitution, a part of the Bill of Rights.

Before we explore this precious but now tarnished gem, let us consider together the nature of our rights. This right, like so many others, has been swallowed whole by Leviathan, not because we have forgotten what this right means but because we have forgotten what a right is. We have forgotten something as simple as the source of a right. Allow me to remind you: a right comes from God. A right is ours by birth. A right is not the state's to give, much less to take away. A right is inalienable; it is natural to us.

Now, some Christians have a problem with this. Doesn't it sound kind of selfish? Aren't we slaves to Christ? Aren't we to turn the other cheek? Such thinking forgets that we are slaves to Christ, the giver of the good gift of liberty. Our fathers went to their deaths because they refused to affirm the lordship of Caesar. The command to turn the other cheek says nothing about turning the cheeks of our wives or our children. Our rights were earned by our King, and we do Him no favor when we despise them, when we throw them away.

We have lost our rights because we worship the god of the state. In Chicago residents of federal housing projects are required to waive their fourth amendment right—that is, they had to sign a waiver allowing searches of their homes with no warrant—in order to secure a home to live in. They turned to the state as their provider first for their housing; then they turned to the same nanny state to do something about the drug problem, whatever it takes to make it stop. And what the state took was their God-given right. We lose our God-given rights when we give God back, and worship the creature rather than the Creator.

Few if any of us live in the projects in Chicago; but we have given over what is ours in lesser ways. We invite the state into our homes when we fill out our tax forms, letting assorted bureaucrats peek through our checkbooks. We invite the state into our homes when we fill out their ridiculous census reports, letting them sniff around our powder rooms. We invite them into our homes when we allow them to come and search our land for wetlands, and then command us on how we may or may not use our land.

I'm not saying we shouldn't do these things. The state is, after all, like the proverbial stick-up man demanding, "More of your money or your privacy." There is no option where you get to keep both. I am saying, however, that we ought to be put out by this state of affairs.

It is not only Uncle Sam who makes himself at home in our homes; we keep an open door for state and local governments as well. In Virginia they still come peeking into our carports to tax us for the cars we've already been taxed on. They also pore over

34

the spending habits of the Sproul clan, to determine how much if any of the money that they've ripped out of my paycheck they will kindly give back.

Then there is the local school district. They come to my house to determine not what I'm spending my money on, but how much my—excuse me, *their*—house is worth. Then they come around for their protection money, otherwise known as property taxes.

Here is where we discover that perhaps the fourth amendment is actually intact. It may simply be that it doesn't apply as I expect, because my home is not only not a castle but it is not mine; I am merely renting it from the state. The same is true for you. If you doubt that the state owns your home, try this little experiment. Don't pay your rent—that is, your property taxes—for a month or two, and see how long it takes for you to be out on your ear, dogged at every step by a bad reference from your 'landlord'. That they control your house, and that they will evict you and sell it if you don't pay them what they say you owe, is proof that they at least believe that it belongs to them.

What can we do? To borrow an analogy from baseball: crowd the plate. We should raise the drawbridge and grow some gators in the moat. Don't let them forget that you at least remember the fourth amendment. If they don't come to your home equipped with a warrant, show them the door, even if you have nothing to hide—*especially* if you have nothing to hide. Let them know at every chance you get who is the King of your castle.

And beseech Him for relief. He is our great King Richard; they are a motley crew of Prince Johns and Sheriffs of Nottingham. Our King will return, and make all things right. He is not only the source of our rights but the source of their power. So as we petition Him for relief, we need to remember that He is already in control. And let us remember that He is preparing for us a castle that no usurper can take away.

As we make our petitions known, let us also know our other rights. We need to exercise our first amendment right to let people know about their fourth amendment right. And the day is coming when we will have to exercise our second amendment right to enforce our fourth amendment right. Perhaps at that point the Common Law will finally become common, and the true law.

CHAPTER 3

Spin

ຂ

*Now the serpent was more cunning
than any beast of the field which
the LORD God had made. And he said
to the woman, "Has God indeed
said, 'You shall not eat of every tree
of the garden'?"*

ఇ

Genesis 3:1

S pin is a diabolical art form. As with opera, as much as I hate it I still at times cannot hide my admiration; there can be a hideous beauty to it. Spin rightly shares with good writing a blurring of the distinction between prose and poetry; but it wrongly blurs the distinction between fact and fiction. That is, I love good spin for its ability to say much with subtlety and with few words; I despise it because what it says is not true.

Poetry is the art of saying very much with very little. It is a form of language that makes use of the fullest extent of the range of meaning in the chosen words. It often evokes more than it communicates. Spin, like good poetry, can leave you guessing, and in that guessing it gives the answers it wants you to find. A good spinmeister feeds you the conclusion in the same way a good magician feeds you the card you thought you were freely choosing. It is the art of making something look like a completely different thing, while also making you think that this is how it has always been.

Would you rather be described as frugal, cheap or a tightwad? Each shares a common theme, but these three different notes reach a different conclusion. The joke becomes far too serious in mass media. Today Gary Condit is a man who has had marital peaks and valleys; forty years ago he would have been a philanderer and a dirty old man; four hundred years ago he would have been an abominable, dead adulterer. Today he gets his picture on the cover of *People;* forty years ago he would have been run out of Washington on a rail; four hundred years ago the rail he was tied to would have been on fire. Spin is what allows the National Organization of (Some) Women to cry for the blood of Clarence Thomas based on allegations of a few crude remarks, and then to cry for compassion when a president is forced by a blue dress to concede an 'inappropriate relationship.'

It is built around the power of words, and their nuances. And the truth of the matter is that we are all guilty, both of spinning and of being spun. We spin when we choose the safe version to describe our own sin. We spin when we choose to describe sins against us in the worst possible light—as having been not just committed but *perpetrated* against us. Such spin is not only a sin against our brothers and sisters, it is also a sin against God. God is the author of language; language means enough to Him that when His Spirit inspired John to write of His Son, he called Him "the Word." Our God is a God who speaks, and therefore He is a God of language. He speaks to us, reveals to us His promises, His warnings, His love for us, and His plan for us—all in words. There are few things that are as precious as words. An assault on the King's English is an assault on the King Himself.

When we spin we are liars. But we then spin ourselves into believing that we are merely learning to be more effective in our communication—and so we lie about our lies. When we spin we treat our fellow image bearers as a bunch of animals that must be manipulated; when we spin we treat truth as a tramp. Although we would never treat the Word contemptuously, we spit on words daily.

As high-handed a sin as spinning is, and as strong a temptation as it is, I believe there is still more mischief in our lives that flows out of still a different sin: failing to discern spin from truth. We are in the mess we are in partly because we either can't or won't seek out the truth. We are spoon-fed the spin of the father of Spin, the devil himself. We accept as true and as normal the spin of the world around us.

What would happen, for instance, if every Christian in the country used the language of the Bible rather than the language of the serpent? How might our own perceptions change, and perhaps even those of the culture around us, if we refused ever to speak of alcoholics and instead called them what the Bible calls them—drunkards? The spin that is the fabric of the culture of victimization, the spin that turns sin into sickness, has found its way into our language—even though we have not, I pray, adopted that worldview.

What would happen if we stopped referring to those who practice a rather peculiar perversion as 'gay' and started instead describing them as sodomites? Oh, but the world would howl at us, and we don't want that, do we? If we use their terms, they hear what they want to hear. *Gay people* are those who were created to love and engage in sexual conduct with members of their own sex; *sodomites*, on the other hand, are perverts whose hatred of God has driven them to sexual insanity. Now which one is it? When we use their term we affirm their conclusions.

The frightening thing about spin is that the more we accept it, the more we can expect of it; the purveyors of spin just get increasingly bold. For example, this past Labor Day holiday the local newspaper cheerily told us that there would be a number of peace officers along the area's roads to perform safety checks. Perhaps you've been through these before. The officer invites you to roll down your window and—for the sake of safety—asks to see your license and registration.

Friends, this is not a safety check; this is nothing more than checking to see if our travel papers are in order, the practice of internal passports. But because it is Officer Friendly and not some Gestapo sadist dressed all in black, we think this is different. Our children, if we send them over to the neighborhood school, will be asked to stand and give a loyalty oath to the state—but we call it patriotism. We call it the pledge of allegiance. If we understood what was happening, surely we wouldn't put up with it, would we? But we have become so spun that when someone speaks the truth to us in plain language, it jars our ears and causes them to close. Straight talk becomes understood as harsh rhetoric.

We invite the state—and their propagandists, the media—to hypnotize us; their verbal spin is like a spinning pocket-watch that puts us to sleep and removes all our worries. And then we not only believe the spin, we start spinning it ourselves. We not only fail to protest when they call socialism 'compassionate conservatism,' we become *passionate* compassionate conservatives.

Recognizing that spin has us imprisoned is only the beginning of the remedy. Now that we recognize its grip on us, how shall we escape that grip? How do we stop our ears, our tongues, our heads from spinning in a spin-crazy world? The answer is surprisingly simple.

First: when we listen, we must translate. We have to understand that they are using a different language, and that as a result it is necessary for us to do the work of translation. When the news reports something about public schools, we must train our minds to tell us: *government schools*. See how easy?

Second: we must spend less time immersed in the language that we are trying to escape. The more time you spend immersed in a language, the more you will begin to think in that language rather than in your native tongue—and, of course, the better you will be able to speak the language. Begin by turning off the TV, so as to avert your eyes from the most pervasive form of spin, advertising. More than any other 'art' form, advertising debases the language and creates verbal inflation.

But in addition to escaping the grip of spin, we need to practice the language of heaven. We need to immerse ourselves in its culture, speak its language, learn its idioms. When we come to the Word of God we find it to be not only true but trustworthy. The fact that President Clinton had an inappropriate relationship with that woman, Miss Lewinsky, is true enough—but it is not at all trustworthy. Such an admission may be true, but it conceals more than it reveals. The Bible does not seek to manipulate us but to guide us into all truth. It makes full use of assorted literary forms, but to enlighten, not to deceive.

It is my hope and desire that in these pages I will avoid this malignant disease, this sin against language. I do speak with vigor. I am not shy about my convictions. But my convictions include the conviction that I must speak truthfully. When the world smooths out the edges, I do not begin to sharpen them. I do not take that hypnotizing spinning watch and spin it in the other direction. I try to tell the truth. That is part of what I mean by being simple. When we are simple, we mean what we say and we say what we mean; there is no need to translate.

To the degree that we succeed at being simple, we also succeed at being separate. What frustrates me greatly is that the evangelical world has done so little to heal its wounds, that we evangelicals think we are separate because we use spin in the service of good. We do not recognize that we must not only eschew the folly of our enemies, but also refuse to use their diabolical tools. The church too often tries to tell the truth with lies; we ought to tell the truth truthfully. We don't need to manipulate people. We don't *want* to manipulate people, for to do so is to fight our own cause; to do so is to lead people to become not only less simple and less separate, but less deliberate.

Which is really what we are talking about. We are not deliberate when we allow the unspoken assumptions in the language of those around us—and in our own language—to color our conclusions or our convictions. When we allow that, we end up being led around by the nose like children; we are tossed to and fro by every wind of doctrine, even when we are utterly unaware that the wind is even blowing. We join in our victim culture, and in so doing become victims of our culture.

But when we are deliberate we have ears to hear, ears to discern the very lies of the father of lies, who is more crafty than any of the beasts of the field. When we are deliberate we find ourselves truly living in that most powerful of words, freedom. We act thoughtfully. We escape the lemming herd.

The right use of words is exactly what it takes to build the kingdom of God. When Paul speaks of our warfare he is not using inflammatory rhetoric, but is carefully speaking the truth. And when he tells us that the weapons of our warfare are not carnal, he is not only not denying that the war is real but is telling us that our weapons are ideas, and, through those ideas, words. Words are our weapons in the fight—which is precisely why what we do at the Highland Study Center is write, read, and talk. And every failure to use words rightly is not only foolish and wicked but is treason. The prayer that accompanies every thing we at the Center produce is that we will be yet another quartermaster in this great war, that we will equip you to be a mighty warrior in the building of His kingdom—not for your glory, not for ours, but for His. Our prayer is that as you read what we write you will be emboldened for that war, not by propaganda but by the truth. Our prayer is that we will together tear down the strongholds of those principalities and powers that have taken control of not just our world, but our minds and our tongues. Our prayer, as always, is that our writings will help you to take every thought captive.

Inflation is not as complicated a monster as politicians want to make it appear. Back in the ancient reign of Gerald Ford we were treated to an interesting campaign to stop the swift rise in prices. People took the President's advice and wore little pins with the letters WIN printed on them. WIN, in case you don't remember, stood for "Whip inflation now." We were spun to believe that prices were rising because greedy sellers wanted more money, and because foolish consumers weren't careful enough with their money. WIN, of course, lost. Inflation is not rising prices any more than smoke is fire. Prices rise as a result of inflation. Inflation is the increasing of the money supply. There are many ways to increase the money supply, but those various shades have nothing to do with my point; however the money supply is inflated, the result is that each existing dollar is diminished—it can no longer carry the freight it once could.

Imagine, if you would, a teeny tiny little economy, one in which the only goods available to buy are ten loaves of bread. Imagine now that this economy had circulating in it ten federal reserve notes. How much does a loaf of bread cost? One dollar—or, for accuracy's sake, one federal reserve note (FRN).

Finally, imagine that Alan Greenspan buzzes over our little economy and drops down ten more FRNs. Everyone is suddenly rich, right? But before you start to celebrate, let me ask you this: how much does a loaf of bread now cost? Right—two FRNs.

Each FRN carries only half its weight now; its buying power has shrunk by half.

I haven't forgotten the subject of this chapter. I haven't gotten dizzy from all this spinning and decided to write a section dedicated to economics. I am instead trying to make a point about language in our age. We live in a culture that is, thanks to the work of spin, beset with language inflation. There is an increasing distance between the words we use and the things they describe. While the nation has yet to experience hyper-inflation, its inhabitants all live in the midst of hype-driven inflation.

It isn't enough anymore for an athlete to give all he has for the team; it isn't even enough for him to give *more* than all he has. Now he has to give 150% in order to avoid being called a slacker. Our stores no longer have sales; now they have mega-sales, sales of the century, super-stupendous, the-earth-will-fall-off-its-axis sales. And for good reason! After all, at these sales you can buy toasters that will make you the happiest person to ever walk the planet. You can save on after-shave that will make you smell better than the home-baked cookies of the gods. You can get a colossal size box of detergent that will have your stains screaming for mercy. And don't get me started on cars being sold like candy bars and towns being invaded by monster trucks.

The problem is not isolated to Madison Avenue. We cannot escape language inflation merely by turning off the television— though that is probably a good idea. While it is Alan Greenspan and his ilk who inflate the money supply, the diminished dollars still trickle down to our own piddling little piles of dough. In like manner the media elite are destroying the very language that we use, leaving us with tired, shriveled words that can't do what they once did—and we respond by making the situation worse.

Rather than be guilty of damning a friend with faint praise, we escalate. "R.C., that was the greatest sermon I have ever heard in all of my life!" (Okay, I have never actually heard this one— but doesn't it work well to illustrate the point?) Here is a mythical person who has learned from the sermon I have preached. He has grown in grace. He wants to communicate to me his appreciation for my work. But if he merely shakes my hand at the end of the service and says, "Thanks, that sermon was good", I'll go away worrying that I have done a pathetic job. If my wife tries to comfort me by saying, "Relax, you did fine", I'll know I stunk up the joint. (She, of course, would have the wisdom instead to say, "Stop worrying about yourself, you self-interested slob", and would not in the least be guilty of word inflation.) Worse still, I will years later describe this pathetic little pity party as my "dark night of the soul."

I'm at all not suggesting that we adopt a stoic pose and act as if nothing matters; I am suggesting that we need to understand that words matter. I'm not making a case for English understatement either; instead I'm asking that we cultivate golden tongues, that our words might ring true and be steady and dependable. If you are hungry, then don't be afraid to make public note of it—but do not cry wolf by announcing that you will expire if you do not eat within the next five minutes. If you are happy, then by all means enjoy a smile, whistle a nice tune—but do not announce that you have been to visit seventh heaven. If you are angry and have a right to be so, then be angry—but please avoid an all-consuming rage because someone "stole" your parking space at the mall.

And forego using the expression "to die for"—unless you are talking about Jesus. Be excited about Jesus, but don't think He is more honored by your singing fifteen verses of *Shine Jesus Shine* than He would be by your singing the Doxology. He won't go away sad if you leave off the fifteenth really of "You are really, really, really, really, really, really, really, really, really, really, really, really, really, really, *really* great, Jesus!" In fact, I think after the first or second one He might just get really, *really* annoyed.

Invest in your words wisely. And if we all do it—well, we won't usher in the millennium, but we might just WWIN— Whip Word Inflation Now.

W hat can I, one puny little speck of dust, do to sway the outcome of this titanic struggle between the forces of good and evil when our enemies are more powerful than a locomotive? How can I hope to stay the onrushing waters of postmodernism?

Step one: take a deep breath. Yes, I am concerned at the subtle assaults that are made on our language every day. I affirm that this battle is part of a larger war that not only will make history but *is* history. But I also deny that this is anything worth hyperventilating over. I do not want to over-hype the problem of hype, or spin myself and my readers as being the last great hope in the battle against spin. What follows are a handful of practical suggestions as to how to be better men of our words, how to more effectively honor our language, how to better obey the ninth commandment in all its fullness.

Write deliberately. Once we lived in a world of paper and ink; now we live in the gnostic realm of the binary universe. Touch a few buttons, and off go my words. Touch a few more, and I make sure I have spelled 'more' correctly. Hit *send*, and like the proverbial arrow, off it goes.

The internet has made publishers of us all, and made us all forget James' wisdom that few should fancy themselves teachers. With paper and ink people actually took their time with what they wrote. They deliberated, mulled. Putting down words took commitment. Now it takes a couple of wires. I see this viscerally in the hate mail that I receive from time to time. I get hand written letters occasionally grumbling about this failure or that of mine, but for real heat and venom it takes an email. The words flow with the passion of the moment and, before you know it—I've got mail.

To combat this tendency, use this rule: if what you have to say to a brother is not worth the trouble of an envelope and a stamp, don't bother saying it.

Speak deliberately. My friend Jonathan Daugherty has a peculiar cadence to his speech. Though he had lived nearby less than a week, I noticed that I had picked it up even without trying. Jonathan talks like my wife Denise eats—slowly. He stops mid-sentence to see if he has the right word, and then stops mid-word just to make sure. With the possible exception of his assessment of Béla Fleck and the Flecktones, I don't believe I've ever heard him exaggerate.

We should all be so careful. No, our spoken words are not written down, but typically they are remembered long after the things we write. Choose them thoughtfully.

Think deliberately. Sometimes the problem isn't just word inflation but *feeling* inflation. Having spent our lives having our emotions whipped into assorted frenzies by our media masters, we somehow feel that unless we are feeling strongly, we aren't really feeling at all. We get an addict's high from the trauma of drama in our lives. We move from "Gee, so and so didn't wave at me at the mall. I wonder if she saw me?" to "Gee, so and so really must think she's something, being too good to wave at me at the mall!" to "I WILL DESTROY SO-AND-SO'S PATHETIC EXCUSE FOR A LIFE IT IS THE LAST THING I DO!" faster than I can think of something that is really fast.

We may all be junior high girls at heart, but we must resist the urge to respond to events as such. And we must resist not only in the events of our day-to-day lives, but also in the events of the world around us. The actor Alec Baldwin promised us that he would leave the country if George W. Bush were elected president. I too hoped it wouldn't happen; I'm terribly disturbed by many things that President Bush is now doing. But George W. Bush was elected and the world did not come to an end— just as it would not have ended had Al Gore been elected.

Let us resolve to stop characterizing each and every day as the great pivot of history.

Listen deliberately. In the last minute or so of reading this wisdom perhaps you have matured. Perhaps you have greater self-control. But soon you will return to a world that has committed the unfathomable folly of not reading this wisdom. And so they will spin and hype, and when they're not hyping they will spin. When they stop spinning, they will hype.

Learn to discern the weasel words, those little fillers that make all the difference. If I said "This is the greatest chapter that has ever been written", your antennae would go up. If, however, I said merely "This chapter is one of the greatest ever written," you might not be alarmed that I had overstepped myself, and might think the better of it. That's what they count on.

Treat the hype and the spin for what it is—so many weeds at which to hack away. Continue hacking at them until you can actually discern whether the message within is a sweet, sweet rose, or just another stinkweed to be hacked to bits.

Read deliberately. As we become a more image-based culture, even our language becomes more image-based. Writers now prefer to paint you a word picture that will get you to emote, rather than carefully making an argument that will get you to think.

Don't play along. Train yourself to recognize the difference by reading some of the old masters. You'll discover that writers in days past were able to communicate without the use of speakers turned up to eleven. You'll find that those writers employed a completely different language, one that communicates powerfully without draining power from itself. You'll find that truly beautiful language is not filled with hype, but filled with truth and delicacy.

And when you must read things that were written recently, use the lessons you've learned from the old masters to sift through the chaff of word pictures as you search for grains of reasoned argument. Such grains are increasingly rare, but they are there to be found.

CHAPTER 4

To a Thousand Generations

ಎ

These things I have spoken to you,
that in Me you may have peace.
In the world you will have tribulation;
but be of good cheer, I have
overcome the world.

ೞ

Philippians 4:8

As I write this I'm on my way home from a homeschooling conference. But my flight has been delayed; instead of getting home late tonight, I'll be home tomorrow morning—late development, afternoon—later still development, night. Instead of spending my evening in a plane, I'm spending it at the airport. Instead of sleeping in my bed tonight I'll be sleeping, if God should so bless, on an airplane.

The dichotomy between the encouragement I receive in being with homeschooling families and the discouragement I feel in being stuck far from my own family is enough to make me eschatologically schizophrenic. On the one hand, within the church we are seeing not only the hearts of fathers returning to their children, but also a slow erosion of the influence of the greatest weapon the devil has wielded against God's people in the last one hundred years—the government school system. On the other hand, I can't even get home on the same day I began my travels. Are we moving forward or backward?

The church at large has been guilty of embracing particular eschatological views depending on its mood. When the world was giddy with enlightenment optimism, when every day in every way the world seemed to get better and better, the church hopped on the happiness bandwagon and embraced postmillennialism. And then when the bulbs of the enlightenment begin to dim, the dim-bulb church hurtled headlong into pessimillennialism. Leading the lemming charge were the dispensationalists; they found in their Bibles reasons for the dread that was within them.

I am schizophrenic about dispensationalism. In the midst of the Fundamentalist-Modernist controversy, the dispensationalists wore the white hats. They stood on the inerrancy of the Bible, affirming the supernatural. And they did so in a way that again pulls me in two directions. On the one hand I am embarrassed by the lack of sophistication among these heroes. These were not officious scholars, careful to dress the academic part. They talked with accents, and often with bad grammar. They wore fat ties. Beside the cool erudition of the mainline liberals they looked like redneck fools—and for that I also love them. Once upon a time they exhibited a supreme indifference toward the approval of their enemies; they were fools for Christ, as we all should be.

While their commitment to the authority of Scripture was then and is now exemplary, their understanding of the Scripture was then and is now severely lacking. Indeed, while they affirmed that all of Scripture was God-breathed, they—at least implicitly—denied that all of it was profitable. They became practical Marcionites, excising huge portions of the Bible—including the whole of the Old Testament, except for those as-yet-unfulfilled prophecies—as no longer applicable to them. That was for another age. And we are under grace. Many even excluded the gospels from their thinking, as the gospels were written prior to the advent of the church age in which they say we now live. They therefore had their own brand of schizophrenia, affirming the truth of the Bible but denying its applicability to us.

The results were more calamitous than their visions of the tribulation. In wrongly dividing the people of God, in driving a wedge between Israel and the church, they cut their followers off from their own history. If we are living in the parenthesis, we are living outside the very stream of history. We cannot know who we are, because we are the great mystery. Because the old covenant did not speak *of* us, it does not speak *to* us.

And so we lost not only our history, we lost our future as well. Those promises are not *our* promises; *we* are only promised that we will miss the greatest battle of history—that we will be sidelined. Indeed, we are already sidelined. We were once not a people, 1 Peter tells us, but we became a people. And now Darby and Scofield and Ryrie tell us we are once more not a people.

With no history and no promise, we likewise have no job to do. We are not really a part of the family of God, just surprise visitors. All we are called to do is to wait. We are merely guests in the kingdom, not co-laborers. And therein is the scent of the devil.

While dispensationalists are experts at sniffing out assorted conspiracy theories, where there is a bogeyman under every bush that will usher in the one world government—or at least serve as fodder for another best selling prophecy book—they miss this great conspiracy. The best way to track a conspiracy is to follow the money, to always ask that probing question: *Cui bono?*—who benefits?

If you are the devil, you are the enemy of the kingdom of God. Your desire is to see it stopped, to thwart its growth. You know that the King has purposed to grow His kingdom through the work of His subjects. You've already infiltrated the mainline churches and caused a retreat of that same Spirit who cried out "Ichabod." But the Spirit has continued to work, giving life, regenerating more soldiers. You can't stop the Spirit, for He blows where He will. What do you do?

What you do is construct a worldview that will demoralize the troops. If you can persuade them that they will lose the battle, they will assuredly lose the battle. If you can persuade them that their Commander has ordained that they would lose the battle, they will throw down their weapons with force. If you can persuade them that they will be sent stateside before the battle really heats up, they'll turn their helmets upside down, set their rumps on them—and wait.

In this the devil has succeeded. He has persuaded the evangel-ical church that the sooner we lose, the sooner Jesus comes back. Every effort we make to make known the kingdom of Christ merely delays the consummation of the kingdom of Christ. Who benefits? The devil. He has paved the road to Dallas.

But there are other beneficiaries as well, or so it would appear; the devil did not have to sweat to make this sale. In his *The Man Who Was Thursday*, G.K. Chesterton recounts a conversation between the recruiter for a secret police force which is fighting a vast conspiracy of anarchists, and Syme, a potential recruit.

"Are you the new recruit?" asked the invisible chief, who seemed to have heard all about it. "Alright, you are engaged."

Syme, quite swept off his feet, made a feeble fight against this irrevocable phrase.

"I really have no experience," he began.

"No one has any experience," said the other, "of the battle of Armageddon."

"But I really am unfit—"

"You are willing, that is enough," said the unknown.

"Well, really," said Syme, "I don't know any profession of which mere willingness is the final test."

"I do," said the other, "—martyrs. I am condemning you to death. Good day."

Christ, the Captain of the armies of the Lord, has called us to battle. He bids us to pick up our cross daily. He tells us that just as He was persecuted, so will we be. But the devil, in his conspiracy of dispensationalism, has declared us all 4-F, unfit to fight in the battle. And he has gone farther, suggesting that the battle is not even ours; it is strictly a matter for the Jews.

The irony is that this otherworldliness—this view that tells us this world is not our home, we're just a-passing through—turns on us and creates worldliness. Because we have no call to purify the world, to sanctify the world, we have no real call to purify ourselves, and so we become colored by the world. We find ourselves watching the movie while we wait for Godot; we pass the time down at Vanity Fair.

And why not? We live under grace, not under law. The world, meanwhile, sinks lower into the muck. The salt has lost its savor, and so the meat has begun to turn green, and we are trampled under foot. Remember that when the devil coaxed us into laying down our arms, he did not lay down his own. Cowards not only do not win the war, they are overrun by the enemy.

At the same time, the world continues to follow the church. The world has embraced lawlessness because the church has embraced lawlessness. We have carnal presidents because we have carnal "Christians." We have a culture saturated with ennui because we too are bored, waiting for the end to come.

It all begins with that schizophrenic view of Scripture. They want us to interpret the Bible literally, but within the grid of a system so obtuse that it takes a million charts to explain it. They want to affirm inerrancy but deny applicability. They want us to take the plain sense of the text, yet they build their eschatology around a word that appears to have been raptured right out of my Bible. They claim to be simple country preachers, but they preach Mr. Scofield's notes instead of the Word that those notes supposedly explain.

We who are Reformed share a great deal in common with dispensationalists. We have the same zeal for the Bible—but we have a zeal for the whole of it. We have the same rejection of assorted Pelagian schemes, whether Romish or liberal—but we also reject the Pelagian taint of Arminianism. We have the same love of God's grace—but we, by His grace and in accordance with His law, also love His law.

For all that we have in common, however, there is this difference: we are fighting to build Christ's kingdom and they are not. They are not only deserters but they teach others to mimic their cowardice. We, not they, come to the text simply. When Christ says "Seek ye first the kingdom of God" that is exactly what we will strive to do. When Christ says, "Behold I have overcome the world," we believe Him and act accordingly. When Christ says we are to be "more than conquerors," we take up our sword and move forward. When Christ says, "Not one jot or tittle of the law will pass away," we refuse to expunge His law from our lives. We, not they, take Him at His word.

While they are losing the battle with a defeatist worldliness, we are seeking to win the battle with an otherworldliness of conquest. We do not separate to wait, but to win. We do not seek to drag the lost on to our lifeboat, but to draw them to the city we are building upon the holy hill of Zion. We seek to let our light shine before men by being set apart from the darkness.

While they blindly follow their 200-year-old tradition, we seek to be deliberate. We want to think through the issues of our day, of our lives, with the aid of the great saints through all of church history—but with our consciences held captive by the word of God alone. We do not want to inherit a system; we want to inherit the riches of revelation of our God, and to inherit the promises that He made to our fathers, the children of Israel.

We ought to strive to be simple in order to build the kingdom of God. We ought to strive to be separate in order to build the kingdom of God. We ought to be deliberate ultimately in this: striving to be sure that everything we do, everything we say, everything we think, and everything we feel—all of it serves the purpose of building the kingdom of God. We have set out to win, through the power of our King, and for the glory of our King; and those who should be our brothers-in-arms, while they may be our brothers, have laid down their arms. May the great Warrior God that we serve see fit to give the dispensational church a Patton-esque slap on the face, and send them out to join the battle.

Only the fool living under the sun determines to "Eat, drink and be merry, for tomorrow we die." What then do we make of those under the Son who claim, "Evangelize, evangelize, evangelize, for tomorrow we are raptured?"

No one wants to come out against evangelism, especially me. It may very well be that in the providence of God the threat of an impending rapture, and of a tribulation to follow, may actually have motivated a few folks to spread the Good News. Wouldn't it just be like God to use such a thing to bring His sheep into His fold? There's a true sign of the sovereignty of God—He is strong enough to use even a dispensational eschatology for His glory. On the other hand, it may be that one day all their apologetical labors will fall on deaf ears when they come to be seen by the world as those whose patron saint is Chicken Little.

That He can use our folly, however, is not an invitation to practice still more folly. We do not want to be foolish all the more that wisdom might abound. Folly has a way of slithering from our hands and biting us on the hind quarters. Wisdom, I believe, requires that we think ahead for thousands of years, that we make plans for this work of making manifest the kingdom of God. Wisdom means working for the long haul.

I am a postmillennialist, meaning that I believe the church of Christ will experience a thousand-year golden age before Jesus returns to make all things right. Despite holding that strong conviction, I pray regularly: *Maranatha, Lord Jesus*, imploring the King to come now. I am pretty sure, though, that this prayer will not be answered—not because of my eschatology but because of the promises of God.

God tells the children of Israel in Exodus 20 that if they will refrain from idolatrous worship, He will bless them to a thousand generations. The literalist dispensationalists, of course, do not think that 'thousand' literally means 'thousand'. It is a symbolic number, they say. And they may be right. But if so it symbolizes a large number, not a small one. He may return after more than a thousand generations. Or it may be a round number, and He may return after only 951 generations. Either way, if a generation is roughly forty years, that means He'll be back somewhere around 39,000 AD— three down, thirty-seven to go. If, on the other hand, He comes tomorrow, 1000 must symbolize roughly 75.

Will the Son of Man find faith on the earth when He returns? He will if I can help it. Here is where the eschatological rubber meets the applicational road: because I believe that He will not come tomorrow, I labor to prepare for His distant coming—not by making scary movies about what could happen tomorrow, but by raising up godly seed. I am raising my children to participate in victory, not to snatch escape from the jaws of defeat.

A Reformed perspective is a transgenerational one, a view of a future that moves forward generation by generation, with each generation not only witnessing the growth of the kingdom but taking part in bringing the growth to pass. The children of dispensationalists sit in their Sunday school classes dreaming about airplanes with raptured pilots; our children are in constant training for the spiritual warfare to which they have been called.

If God should bless Denise and me with more covenant children, and if He should in turn bless our children's labors as they raise our grandchildren in the nurture and admonition of the Lord, and if He should bless those children as well with quivers full of mighty weapons, and such should continue for thousands of years, for hundreds of generations—what might this world look like? How might our King's glory shine forth before the watching world? Dispensationalists are forever warning us about polishing the brass on the Titanic because they don't realize that we are building the Starship Enterprise—or, rather, that we are polishing spaceship Earth as we prepare for the return of the King.

Most of you have heard the multi-level marketing spiel before, about the wisdom of taking slices of the fruit of the labor of a thousand people rather than merely laboring for your own fruit. While that might be a pipe dream when it comes to friend-nagging home businesses, it is the substance of the business of our homes. I love my children madly, as they are here and now; but I dream of the day when they will be the great-great-grandparents of several thousand godly grandparents. I want my 'downline' filled to capacity with fearless soldiers. You can neither have such a dream nor achieve such a dream if your vision of the future is that it will all end in failure tomorrow.

I am not suggesting that dispensationalists make bad parents; I'm sure many of them would put me to shame. I am suggesting, however, that their labors do not match their own system—and that there are no doubt many whose labors—or lack thereof—*do* match their system. A vision spanning hundreds of generations cannot thrive in the soil of pessimism. You will have trouble raising godly seed under the clouds of doom.

The biblical vision, however, can inspire us to obedience. When we know the kingdom will grow, when we know that God is faithful in His covenants, when we know that He has promised to be God to us, to our children, and to as many as are afar off, when we know that Christ not only came to conquer the world but that He has *already* overcome it—then we move forward in the faith. We move forward believing the good news of the Kingdom of Christ. We don't send our little children out to drag their heathen classmates onto the boat; we prepare them for the larger task of raising their own children to be a light to a world that is not triumphing but perishing. Eschatology then becomes more than a theological parlor game. It is the very spring in our step, the very hope that is within us, the very vision that we are to pass onto His blessings—that He is in the midst of blessing to a thousand generations.

Our peculiar vision at the Highlands Study Center, like politics, can make for some strange bedfellows. On our left are those who share our desire for influencing the world. These are the friends who view serving on the local school board or canvassing the neighborhood on behalf of some political candidate as service to the King. These are the folks whose love for the lost drives them to adopt their manners and mores. These are the well-heeled visionaries who think that if Christians will only spend enough money making a movie then Christianity will take over the world.

We at the Center, however, do not want simply to influence the world, we want to take it over. We don't want a place at the table; we want everyone to recognize that the table belongs to Jesus alone. And what separates us from these well dressed corporate boys for Christ is our strategy of separation. We conquer by retreat. We build bridges by building walls. We win the world by living in another world.

We at the Center also share with dispensationalist friends on our right the notion of *antithesis*—the idea that we are a set-apart people, that the world around us is hell-bent on hell. We don't want to be tainted with the cooties of the culture around us. The trouble is that our compatriots on this side of the aisle are not fighting the war. They have already given up the table. Some even deny that it belongs to Jesus. There is a gnostic strain in dispensationalism, a spiritualism that is deadly and selfish.

The culture around us is awash in sin; it is overripe and in need of a bath. And, for the sake of the elect, we need to give it a bath. We rightly see the world as our enemy, but we must rightly love them as our enemy. The left wing of the church fails at the beginning of that equation; the right wing fails at the end. Loving our enemies requires not simply that we warn them that this world is about to explode, but that we also labor to stomp out the fuse. We need to work for a world where we can tell them of another world. And that is one more way in which dispensationalism falls short.

It is fuel for the fire to point out that western culture is in radical decline. I do not deny it. I recognize that things are getting ugly in the world—precisely because they are already ugly in the church. When another teenage gunman treating his school like a video game is greeted with a yawn, when sodomites become a protected class, when a million and a half babies are killed every year, we can safely conclude that the salt has lost its savor. And perhaps it has lost its savor because the left wing of the church has decided it will do a better job as salt if it pretends it is meat, while the right wing spends its time imploring the meat to hurry up and turn to salt before the destruction comes.

I don't want the world to fall apart, for it yet contains those who will be called out of the world. I wish peace upon the prince of Babylon because I want us free to make manifest the reign of the Prince of Peace. The ingathering of Pentecost could not have happened forty years later, when all Jerusalem was under siege and at each other's throats. The preacher will have a hard time gathering an audience when Attila the Hun is rampaging through town. And in our time a million and a half sinners go to their death each year having never heard the gospel. That is why we are called to be salt and light—that we might preserve the peace so that the elect might be embraced by the light.

I don't know the future. It is possible in the providence of God that western culture will experience revival such as the world has never seen. It is possible that these United States will once again become a free nation, one that gladly kisses the Son. It is possible that the kingdom will enjoy steady growth from today forward. But it sure doesn't look that way. It is more likely that we as a culture will go the way of all flesh.

One thing I am certain of, however—that all that we do to build the kingdom will not return void. I'm certain that if we are faithful stewards, the Master will reward us. I'm sure that if God has called us to polish the brass on the Titanic, then when He returns the brass will be raised from the deep and put to use along with the rest. Nothing will be wasted. That which we as salt preserve will last forever.

It is a good thing both to pray for the peace of Babylon and to work for it. It is a good thing not only for us but for those who are lost and perishing. Our love for the world must not be a love of attraction, a love that yearns to embrace the world; it must be a love of compassion, a love that wants to see the world redeemed. If we can manage that, we can labor for the world without becoming like it. If we can manage that, then we will be salt and light.

Those on the left accuse us of being retreatists; they tell us we do not care for the lost. Those on the right accuse us of being worldly; they tell us that we have forgotten about heaven. We bear these accusations with pride. Our accusers on our left are the worldly ones; our accusers on the right are the retreatists. We strive to be neither, but instead to be faithful citizens of the kingdom of heaven, for the glory of the King, and for the sake of the citizens of Babylon. For such were all of us.

CHAPTER

Baseball

෨

*Finally, brethren, whatever things are
true, whatever things are noble,
whatever things are just, whatever things
are pure, whatever things are lovely,
whatever things are of good report,
if there is any virtue and if there
is anything praiseworthy—meditate
on these things.*

ೞ

John 16:33

Try to imagine the frustration inherent in being a loser. You may take some comfort in knowing that there are countless other losers—but what really gets your goat is the constant winners. Only a *loser* loser takes comfort in company. You set your sights on the winners, work your heart out, spend yourself in the fields of glory—and find yourself on the losing end of the score. (If you find it difficult to imagine such a thing, I cordially invite you to come and challenge the reigning Highlands Study Center darts champion for a taste.)

Joe Hardy spent a lifetime as a loser. Year after year he watched as his beloved Washington Senators—that's the baseball team; one would have to be a loser indeed to love the politicians—missed out on winning the pennant. The Yankees stood in their way and could not be moved.

The devil saw here an opportunity. Joe was an old man, but the devil offered to make him young again, to gift him with a mighty bat, and to make him an unbeatable force for the Senators. And all Joe had to give up in return was his soul. Such is the premise behind a Broadway musical called *D@#n Yankees*; I have never seen it, but its name has crossed my mind if not my lips from time to time.

Let me try one more time to clarify my understanding of Yankees without putting my foot in my mouth. There are lots of different ways to use the term. Yankees can merely describe soldiers in the northern army during the late unpleasantness; those Yankees are dead. Yankees can also describe a baseball team; these I can basically take or leave. Yankees can also describe people who are or were born north of the Mason-Dixon line; I love these folks, because they include my parents, my sister, my cousins, my grandparents, my wife, myself—and, I'm sure, many of you. Please understand that I am not addressing these folks when I talk bad about Yankees.

Last there is our family definition, a definition that revolves around a worldview. They are universal, while we are local. They are unitarian, while we are trinitarian. They are statists, while we are states' rightists. They are individualistic, while we are communitarian. They are industrial, while we are agrarian. They are egalitarian, while we are hierarchical. Yankees are those people who are rude, pushy, and like to live in the city instead of the country.

When I speak bad about Yankees, I'm talking about those who hold to that particular ideology; I'm not fussing at those who merely like to live in the city, nor am I saying that the above describes all people living in the north, nor that all those who live in the south uphold the ideals listed above. I do think that there are more of us down here, and more of them up there. But if you aren't a unitarian, statist, centrist, industrialist, individualist, egalitarian person, I'm not talking about you. The world is full of fine folks up north, just as we still have hordes of Yankees living down here. In fact, *Yankees* is a gentler term for these folks than what I'd like to use; as is so often the case, when people think I'm being blunt, I'm actually toning it down.

In the previous chapter I went toe to toe with that system of theology which is always winning the pennant with its message of losing the World Series, dispensationalism. I argued that a pessimistic view of the future is at odds with the Bible, and with the sovereignty of God. I have received letters and emails and have been in conversations in which others have wondered if maybe I have my head in the sand, if maybe I am an umpire in need of some new glasses.

We are retreating in the battle to build the kingdom of God. We, like our southern forbears, are indeed overrun by Yankees. We had more Christians martyred for the faith in the twentieth century than we did in all other centuries combined. We have watched the church become more and more like the world. The salt has lost its savor. And the world has become more and more a cesspool of evil and ignorance. The smell of death surrounds us. This is progress? they all want to know.

Yes and no. We need to remember Who is running this game. One of the great things about baseball, even in the midst of the

Yankees heyday, is that one can never tell who might win a game; on any given day either team might win. The team that loses a full third of its games is doing exceedingly well; in like manner, any batter who can hit safely merely one out of every three at bats is a superstar. We can be pretty sure that the Cubs and the Red Sox will not win the World Series—each of those teams has gone more than seventy-five years without winning it all. But we can't be totally sure, can we? In 1951 the then New York Giants entered into the last six or so weeks of the season thirteen and a half games out; from there they went on a tear, while the Dodgers crumbled. They finished the regular season in a tie. The one-game playoff ended when the Giants' Bobby Thompson took Ralph Branca long to end the game. It was called the shot heard 'round the world.

There was a previous shot that earned that moniker, when in the battle of Lexington and Concord a ragtag team of minor leaguers took on the World Champs—and shocked the world by winning. God runs an orderly universe, but every now and again He upsets that order to remind us that He is the one running things. He brought the mighty Egyptian empire to its knees and set free the slaves. Having then brought them to the Promised Land, time and again He delivered victory when the odds were against them. He benched tens of thousands of players before leading Gideon into what looked like an impossible upset. Later still, as the Yankees laid siege to Jerusalem, in the bottom of the ninth, with two outs and two strikes, a few starving lepers headed to the enemy clubhouse hoping for a sip of champagne—only to find the place deserted and the banquet feast laid out.

In like manner He took a crew of tax collectors and fisherman, and made of them "these who have shaken the world." This after He had accomplished His greatest victory with the gruesome death of His champion. When it appeared Rome was on its last legs, He surprised us all and gave life to Constantine, and then victory on the battlefield against all odds. He took a neurotic, dyspeptic monk, and brought the rolling army of Romish clerics to a halt. He took the hapless Mets and made them the Miracle Mets of 1969.

This is the God we worship. He is the unhittable closer and the unstoppable batter. He has the range of Willie Mays and the arm of Roberto Clemente. He is the true Great One. We think that we're losing, that the Yankees will always win, because we don't know God. He delights to lift up the lowly and to bring down the mighty. He not only chooses the winner but He decides when the fat lady will sing.

It is only when we forget Him that we end up blowing the game. We see the failures all around us and decide to take matters into our own hands. We figure, like the 'nobles' of Scotland, that the best approach is to negotiate with the devil. If we can show him our strength, maybe we can at least salvage something. We in effect bench our only power hitter, because He won't play that game.

When we cut a deal with the devil, we cut out the King. We leave Him behind, and then we wonder why the Yankees win year after year. We have dead babies because, instead of being faithful, we cut deals and put faithless men in office. We have Columbines because we were satisfied with being allowed to pray at graduation or before a football game. We tell the world, "We're not asking that the Lordship of Christ be affirmed over education, for goodness' sake. That frightens us as much as it does you. We just want a moment of silence."

The Broadway musical had one thing right. If we want to defeat the Yankees, we do need to sell our souls; there is no hope without this. As long as we hold onto what we are, to what we have, we're playing for the Yankees whether we know it or not. When we sell our souls we receive the promise that not only will we defeat the Yankees but that the postgame celebration will last forever. For we do not sell our souls to the devil but to the Savior, who bought them not with lies but with His life, death and resurrection. We need to recognize not only that we need Him on the field but that we belong to Him. He is the star, the coach, the manager, the umpire and the owner.

Why do we know that the Yankees will go down in defeat? Not because of all that God has done in history; that He has brought to pass surprising victories is no argument that He always will. No, we know it because He has promised it. When I look out over our dying culture I cannot be pessimistic, because He told me to be of good cheer, for He has already overcome the world. We are called to walk by faith and not by sight.

This confidence is part of what I mean by being simple. We need not, in order to determine the future, stick our fingers to the wind or crunch the numbers from the leading cultural indicators. Instead we, like the children we are, must believe our heavenly Father. We must have the utmost confidence in our hero to snatch victory from the jaws of defeat.

This is also part of what I mean by being separate. We do not play the game by the same rules as everyone else. We are set apart by our conviction that the sky is not falling, that all things are as they should be. Our peace passes understanding because it is grounded in the immeasurable sovereignty of God. We do not lose sleep over the fate of the Washington Senators, either the baseball or the political variety, because we cheer for the true home team, the Kingdom of God.

This too is part of what it means to be deliberate. We do not bury our heads in the sand when we affirm that we will win the game. Instead we realize that more trustworthy than any box score is the very Word of God. What it says, we believe— because it is God who is saying it. We do not succumb to panic, nor to depression, because we believe God.

All of these things work together to build the kingdom, as we round those bases and return safely to our home, an Eden that has been remade and that now covers all the world. As we rest, we move forward in victory. As we have peace, we win the war. As we surrender to Christ, He breaks the kneecaps of His enemies—not with a mere bat but with a rod of iron. It is the

Yankees who would be wise to learn to fear us; they should know that the fool who leads them onto fields of glory has been losing for as long as he has been lying. And we are honored to play on this field of dreams.

Someone once said that culture is religion externalized; I would suggest that sport is culture ritualized. As *Gladiator* became the circus of choice in our culture, I couldn't help but wonder why. Did we like watching the Roman culture at its most decadent so that we could feel better about our own culture, or did we like watching Roman culture at its most decadent because we are as decadent as they were?

It is true that neither any real actors nor Russell Crowe were actually hurt during the filming of those scenes; we all knew that. But didn't we pay for the privilege of making a part of ourselves believe that it was real? They didn't just tell us what it was like—they showed us. And we did drink. While the Romans were vicariously bloodthirsty, we are circumspectly bloodthirsty. They liked the show because they enjoyed watching others spill blood; we pretend that we like it for some other reason.

This shift—or decline—in our culture works itself out not only in the movies we watch, but in the sports we watch as well. It was once said that baseball was America's pastime, but we have passed that time. Sure, the revenue is still there. People still go to the games, and a few even listen to the games. But that is fading fast. It's not ultimately scandals and greedy players and greedy owners that are killing the game; instead we are no longer worthy of it.

When men gather around the watercooler at work, or around the pew before church, it is unlikely that we will be talking baseball. We would have talked of nothing else forty years ago. Now we are apt to grunt our way through a conversation on the latest Winston Cup race, or on the latest tag team Texas death match featuring The Rock and Stone Cold Steve Austin against Rowdy

Roddy Piper and Hollywood Hogan, or perhaps on the prospects of our favorite football or hockey team—all of which come with the enticing promise of much blood and pain.

Like the fighting in *Gladiator*, we know the wrestling is as thoroughly fake as China's—uh—parts, but we still tune in. Of course we don't take it seriously. But we do fill the coffers down at Pay-Per-View Inc. We buy the T-shirts; and our children, instead of playing catch, are in the back yard practicing the latest version of the body-slam.

I've heard all the arguments from the NASCAR crowd: we watch because of the skill, the athleticism, the strategy that goes into winning a race; we don't come to watch them crash. To such I ask, "Would you be there if a speed limit of say, 30 m.p.h. were imposed?" That would also take skill, reflexes, strategy, endurance, and concentration; but we like only those nuances which take place against a back drop of potential death. No one cheers at the deftness with which Lance Armstrong changes gears or rides in someone's draft; we don't care at all, because he's riding a ten-pound bicycle instead of a three-thousand-pound, eight-hundred-horsepower casket.

Football is much the same way. Here I'm stepping on my own toes, as I have been unable to give up my affair with the Steelers. I can make the same argument that the NASCAR fans use. Football is like ballet, I say—except what gets *me* out of my chair and dancing like I've just scalped someone is the brutal hit. Watch the highlights sometime; they will show the leaping grab, the graceful return, but for each of those they will show three teeth-jarring hits.

Hockey, of course, has no teeth-jarring hits—because by the time you reach the NHL all your teeth have been placed in jars. Hockey is French-Canadian for "blood on ice." And don't even get me started on the tattooed gangsters and hip-hop stars of the NBA. Whatever our sport of choice, it is all bloodsport. If there's not an ambulance parked out back, we don't want to watch.

But violence is not the only issue. Baseball is no longer our national past time because it doesn't pass time quickly enough. We as a culture are losing our patience with the game of baseball. Baseball is, like no other, a game of strategy, of finesse, of thinking several moves ahead. It is the popular equivalent of chess in a Game Boy age. Baseball is more apt to make us go "Hmmm", than it is to make us go "WOW!" And we want "WOW!". Now the only thing we go "WOW!" about is the salaries. It is not a sign of health that the biggest story—practically the *only* story—of a recent off-season was the contract for one shortstop.

The only thing extreme about the sport of baseball is its cost. And we'd rather talk about the money than the sport. Money is exciting; the sport of baseball, on the other hand is slow, cerebral, and can actually be played by old guys like Nolan Ryan, Cal Ripken Jr. and Mark Dewey.

Baseball is to books what our now-popular sports are to movies. We want flash and dazzle. We don't want to be amused, we want to be amazed. We want that rush of adrenaline, even if we have to borrow it, just like the citizens of Rome. And like Rome in the days of the gladiators, baseball is running out of steam and running on fumes. It survives only because of what it once was. No longer do sons wheedle their fathers to play catch; instead fathers wheedle their sons. As the baby boomers die, so will baseball. They tried an extra hitter, concrete bowls, spandex uniforms and rubber fields to win the next generation. (Thankfully they didn't try Vince McMahon and Jesse Ventura.) And they went hit-less. They have since returned to old-fashioned ballyards, uniforms, and—with their last modicum of wisdom— real grass, peanuts and cracker jack, because the only people who care are those who remember how it used to be.

Where have you gone, Joe DiMaggio? A nation turned its jaundiced eyes from you. Boo hoo hoo.

Christians in the game of baseball enjoy not only the game but their time away from the game. They not only play baseball but talk baseball. From time to time they engage in debate on the ethics of the game. (And a few have even been known to debate the morality of free agency.)

Perhaps the greatest debate is over the use of chin music—the brush-back pitch. Here the pitcher throws high and tight, often dropping the batter to the dust, sometimes plinking them on a shoulder, and sometimes beaning them on the bean. No one argues that it's legitimate to do the latter, but all concede that control is never absolute, and the more inside one pitches, the higher the odds of such an end.

The defense of the brush back is simple and grounded in the law of God. The eighth commandment, some pitchers reason, forbids stealing, and the inside of the plate belongs to the pitcher; a batter crowding the plate is a thief who needs to be punished—or at least reminded whose property he is leaning over. The inside pitch, from this point of view, is merely an enforcement tool of existing law.

There is, however, no deed granting the inside of the plate to the pitcher. The batter isn't squatting on another's land; both the pitcher and the batter claim the same piece of property. Chin music is the result of a dispute over ownership.

Many of the recent high-profile confrontations between the feds and assorted sovereign citizens are grounded in a similar disagreement. The Branch Davidians, Randy Weaver, the Republic of Texas and the Freemen of Montana were guilty of ... exactly what? As far as I can recall, among the whole of them the only crime committed was Weaver's sawing off a shotgun barrel a quarter-inch shorter than the law allows—and then only when an undercover agent asked him to do it.

What actually earned these folks the ire of Uncle Sam was that they crowded the inside of the plate. They got into their scrapes because they refused to bow and scrape. And Uncle Sam doesn't take the time to debate the ethics of chin music.

Those events concern me not because I live in a compound where I rant about the seven seals, nor because I belong to a white supremacist group, nor because I have placed liens on the property of corrupt judges, nor because I have seceded from the union—but because I too want to crowd the plate. I believe that the plate belongs to me. Which puts me in danger, even if I'm not a member of the black helicopter crowd.

In eastern Virginia there is a family much like mine. The Thoburns have been vocal in their convictions about the authority of Christ over all things. They have been politically active. They have run for office, published great books, built God-honoring schools. And now, one of them is in jail. His crime? He didn't plant as many trees as the government told him to plant.

John Thoburn owns a driving range. His father owns property beside the range. And so the state demanded so many trees, so many feet tall, so many feet apart. John Thoburn backed off the plate, because he knew what was up: the state was about to condemn the land to expand a road, and the market value of a failed driving range is much less than that of a thriving business. And, incidentally, the municipality owns a couple of its own driving ranges.

Still, he did what they asked. Then they asked for more—trees, that is. Mr. Thoburn inched closer to the plate and refused. And so he sat in jail for 97 days, charged with contempt of court, until he consented to have the county plant the trees on his property, at an expense of $32,000; that expense was in addition to the $48,500 fine the government levied against him.

Note that the government didn't even bother to find some rare bug on the property to justify their intrusion. They found no evidence of wrongdoing. All it took was one man to claim his God-given fourth amendment right to control his own property and he was carted off to jail.

Note also that you have heard nothing about this. CNN doesn't come around when a judge removes a pastor from his pulpit—Martin Murphy—or when a swat team of T-men storms a home and drags a family off to jail for buying, warehousing and selling silver—Franklin Sanders—or when another judge incarcerates a man for not planting trees—John Thoburn. All these bean balls were hurled while the commercials ran on television. And so it will continue to be.

So what do we do? We crowd the plate. If we give up the inside, they'll contend that the middle of the plate is theirs. Eventually, we'll be standing in the on-deck circle while the feds strike us out one after another. I know the feds have a fastball that can make our head spin. I know what it feels like to take one between the shoulder blades. But the real issue is not whether or not we get beaned, but whether we maintain control of the inside of the plate.

We need to remember that we're holding a bat. We are being brushed back because we are feared. The government doesn't bother come after its slaves, but it must come after free men and women, because we are a threat. When we cease to live as free men, we cease to be a threat. And then there will be no free men.

The bat, the deed to the whole of the plate, even the state's fear—all find their source in Christ our King. We are feared because they fear Him. We are assaulted because they fear Him. And we are able to stand tall because we fear Him. It is He alone who has—as our forefathers reminded us—endowed us with our rights. They come from Him alone, and He alone can take them away.

Stand tall in the batter's box, and know that the glaring monster on the mound is a mound of quivering fear.

CHAPTER 6

Technology

ೞ

*He has made everything beautiful
in its time. Also He has put
eternity in their hearts, except that
no one can find out the work
that God does from beginning to end.*

ೞ

Ecclesiastes 3:11

Dirt amazes me. Like water, there are three forms in which it comes. All things being equal, it is dirt. Add water, and now you have mud. Take all the water out, and there you have dust.

The dust is my original birthplace—*from dust you were formed*—and it will also be my (temporary) end—*and to dust you shall return*. One of the ways I try to help people understand the science of economics, and how it relates to our charge to exercise dominion, is to remind people that everything we have comes from the ground or from the water. The food we eat, the paper we read, the computer on which I am writing—if we trace through the physical origins of anything far enough, we end up back at the dirt.

One nearby church chided passers-by with its sign that read, "Be patient. It takes time for grass to become butter." I needed the patience called for by the sign to figure out what that meant. Grass gets eaten by the cow, the cow turns it into milk, the milk is taken out of the cow and churned, and there you have butter. Go back even further and you see that it was the dirt that fed the grass that nourished the cow that gave birth to the cow that gave the milk.

Books, pictures, light bulbs, pencils, tires—it all goes back to the dirt. The rockets that scratch the surface of space, they are made from the dirt and powered by the dirt, as is the satellite that connects your telephone call. Sooner or later you get back to the dirt.

C.S. Lewis touched a bit on the power of dirt when he wrote on the creation of Narnia. In *The Magician's Nephew* we are given a description of the creation of that world by Aslan. As the Lion sings, the stars appear to dance. Soon light fills the sky, and then the flat earth begins to bubble like so much toasted cheese. Birthed from the earth, out of those bubbles come the animals that would inhabit the land. A little bubble breaks open and out comes a beaver. A big bubble pops and there stands an elephant.

It is the land itself that is brimming with life. Poor hapless Uncle Andrew, with his mop of unruly hair, is mistaken by some new-born animals for a plant, and so is planted in the dirt upside down. His pockets empty of their coins, and what should spring up but a tree of gold and a tree of silver (the story was written back when money was money). The wicked Empress Jadis, who would become the White Witch in later stories, had by mistake dragged the cross-piece of a London street lamp with her to this young world. In her flight from Aslan she drops the piece; it too takes root and—skip the rest of the sentence if you haven't read this great series, and while you're at it, go ahead and give yourself thirty lashes—becomes the lantern made famous in Lantern Waste in *The Lion, the Witch and the Wardrobe*. There was the power of life in the dirt of young Narnia.

I venture to guess that such was the power of the ground on which Adam and Eve trod. Their garden was edenic. They were called to dress and to till the garden, but their labor would not strain them; it would be a joy. The fall changed all that. Look at what God tells Adam as He pronounces His curse on him: "Cursed is the ground for your sake; in toil you shall eat of it all the days of your life. Both thorns and thistles it shall bring forth for you, and you shall eat the herb of the field. In the sweat of your face you shall eat bread till you return to the ground, for out of it you were taken, for dust you are and to dust you shall return" (Genesis 3: 17B-19).

The ground from which had come plenty was now made stingy by the hand of God. The ground which had promised to bring forth only goodness and health was now to be the source of thorns and thistles. Where their labor was once a delight, it was now to be burdensome.

And so it still is. Dirt not only brings us the things we love but the things we despise. Weeds burden our labor, whether they be literal or figurative. The ground feeds both the bugs that infest our homes and the bugs that muddle our computers. As an agrarian wannabe I love the ground; but as with all of God's good gifts between now and the consummation, the ground is a mixed blessing.

The same is true of our focus for this chapter, technology. Though I desire to live a more simple life, I am not a Luddite. I recognize that I get to live out here in the country with chickens for food and wood for heat because of the complex wonder of the computer on which I am now writing; without it I'd be living still in the old technological paradigm, the big city. If we lived in the time of the Luddites—when technology was looked upon with an unnatural suspicion, as if it came from somewhere other than the earth—no doubt my focus here would be to get people to relax, to embrace the greater tools of dominion.

That, however, is not where we are as a culture or as a church. We live in an age of technological wonders, and have lost the capacity to wonder whether all this technology is actually healthy. We are building skyscrapers whose height boggles our mind, such that we have failed to count the cost. Technology is indeed a glory, but it can also be a death trap; it has lawful uses and peculiar temptations. It is, as one thinker has called it, "the God who limps."

In arguing that technology has elements of blessing and yet still carries with it the curse, I am not therefore arguing that it is therefore neutral. Such is an unwarranted but all too common response. When I raise a red flag, the technophiles jump into technological relativism: "Oh, there's nothing wrong with technology. What matters is the way we use it."

Granted, dirt is dirt and technology is technology. I'm not arguing that combines and optical scanners have secret meetings late at night to plan their havoc. Technology is morally neutral, if what we mean by that is technology it is not a moral agent. I'm not arguing like a gnostic that the physical is icky; rather I'm saying that technology comes with its own thorns and thistles, and as such is not an unqualified good.

My concern with the "what matters is the way we use it" crowd is that they miss that technology can sometimes use us as well. Its capacity to dazzle can too easily hide its darker side. We ought to be amazed at the feats of dominion that God has graced us with over the last century or so; but we ought to search out their hidden costs as well.

Every time I ride in an airplane and watch the ground recede, I am astonished. But that same amazing machine makes it easier for me to be away from my family, from my local body.

I can't get over the cellular phone. I can call my friend Laurence wherever he may be and talk over an article I'm writing. I can be traveling down the road and call down to Orlando and talk to my colleagues down there. It's amazing. But what if I use it to keep in touch—without ever actually touching?

On the internet I can search out like-minded people all over the world and visit with them. In the meantime, my thirst for companionship is satisfied—and I never speak to my neighbor.

I'm still astounded that on any given day, I can enjoy the sensation of streams of hot water pouring down my back. I do it without thinking twice about the cost; I can do it twice a day without thinking about the cost. But what if this gift turns me into a sissy, unwilling or unable to bear going a day without it, or undoing the magic of the shower by going out and breaking a sweat doing some real work?

And how might the ease with which I can now write this chapter change the nature of the chapter?

To put it another way, there are strings attached to technology, hidden costs that might be debited from our characters. One small example: my chickens may not lay eggs like the ones down at the Eggs "R" Us egg factory, but then my chickens lay eggs that taste good. My eggs come from chickens, not from the grocery store.

Not only is there a message in the medium, but that message gets through and changes us. Whether I use this computer to research the wisdom of the Puritan divines or look for gossip of the divine Miss M., I'm still hooked into a machine that can give me instant access—which is good, and bad, but never neutral.

This is why we so desperately need to be deliberate about the very habits of our hearts. With the magic of technology buzzing away in the background, it's hard to pay attention to the message. That is perhaps my greatest concern about technology: it can distract us from our first calling. Even though the Harvester 3000 may double the yield of our cornfield, if it helps us forget that we are dependent upon God it is not a tool for dominion but a tool of the devil. If we're humming to the built-in CD player, we may not be enjoying God's gift of musical beauty but using it to distract ourselves, to avoid thinking about beauty as a gift from God.

This is why we at the Highlands Study Center want to live simple lives. We're not against technology as such, any more than we are against dirt. We are wary of it, though, and we want eyes capable of seeing through the fairy dust of technological wonder and souls unstained by the mud of temptation. We don't want to throw ourselves into the briar patch, the thistles of technology. We don't want to find ourselves unable to let go of that tarbaby, becoming addicted to the so-called new and improved.

We at the Center love to exercise dominion, but we don't want technology exercising dominion over us. Too often we become slaves to our technology by judging our lives against technological standards, and working hard not to overcome the thorns and thistles in the dirt but to overcome the mountain of debt we've piled up while buying all the latest gadgets of the day. We at the Center want to be free, to be masters and not slaves.

And such, of course, makes us weird—set apart from the world around us. While they are busy worshipping this limping God of technology, we are zealous for worshipping the true God of the strong right arm. We are a people who are more concerned with joys of a well-earned nap than the legal conundrums of thieving through Napster. We are a people who know the difference between infusion and imputation, but who couldn't tell an MP3 from a Palm VII. Our values are different and so our lives look different. We neither reject a particular technology because of its birth date as the Amish do, nor do we embrace the latest technology simply because it is the latest. We are set apart because we are deliberate. And we are able to be deliberate because we are simple.

Go ahead and throw another log on the fire. Read like reading is supposed to be done, not with a hand on a mouse, not slogging your way through hyperlinks that only serve to make you hyper, but simply. Sit back with the drink of your choice—as long as it is not some industrial sludge—and have a nice read, remembering that real change comes when real people have real conversations about really important things.

Although it is still dark out this morning, I've already begun a productive day. The fire is burning in the next room, the light bulb burns above me giving me light. I have cut Doug Wilson down to size—that is, I've edited the articles he's written for the next two issues of *Tabletalk*. Having done so, I have set my Macintosh computer to work in sending the finished Wilson articles down to my comrades in Orlando, while on my PC I write this chapter for *Eternity in Our Hearts*. (By the way, lest you think I've gone corporate, I also just finished a breakfast of toast made from my wife Denise's home-made bread, which in turn was made from home-ground wheat.) I'm feeling good, feeling strong, everything is just whipping along. Oh—I've got mail. Isn't technology grand?

Technology this morning gives me a feeling of power; I am master of all I survey. I send this here and it goes. I retrieve that from there, and it comes. I push buttons, and behold, my thoughts appear on the screen. I've got it all under control—unless something happens to go wrong.

That feeling of mastery can dissipate faster than the early morning darkness; all it takes is for the cursor to stop blinking, or for one of those weird messages to pop up on my screen—*Warning: Asymptotic COBOL error number 4*—and I'm suddenly

Superman drowning in a pool of liquid kryptonite. Technological hubris is not the exclusive domain of genetic scientists and nuclear physicists; it comes upon all of us when we pridefully assume that we have it all under control. And it happens perhaps most frequently at the point where technology intersects with our families.

There is probably no greater life-changing event than the arrival of a child. Jobs change often. That big mortgage we signed is financing a house that will one day be rubble. But children last forever. Not a one of us would hesitate to burn down our homes or take a third job cleaning sewers if it would keep our children alive. And there is nothing that makes us more flummoxed, makes us feel more helpless, than the birth of a helpless newborn.

This week my young daughters Shannon and Delaney have been sick, and sick in the most unpleasant ways. I want to make them well, but instead all I can do is hold them with one hand and hold a pot in front of them with the other. I am helpless against the invisible bug that assaults them. Even the doctors tell us, "Just wait, they'll get over it."

This helplessness too often does not cure us of our pride. God humbles us, but we are not humbled. We reason that if we can't manage children when they come, at least we can manage when or if they come. The geniuses down at Dow Chemical have put in our hands the power over life and death—or so we think. Sometimes, by the grace of God, our technology of death fails us and God gifts us with a helpless baby.

And at other times, in the judgment of God, our technology of life fails us and we learn the hard way that we never had it under control. Sometimes He rewards our assumption that we are in charge, that we have the power of life in us, by giving us charge and letting us fail.

What would our forefathers have thought had they known that the blessings of their blessings would one day schedule the arrival of blessings as if they were bottles of milk left on the stoop? A soon-to-be-married couple tells themselves, "We figure that we'll spend a few years after the wedding getting to know each other, just the two of us, and working so we can save money for a house. Then we'll have our first child, and when he turns four, then we'll start working on the next. If at that point we have one of each then we'll probably just quit, and then five years after that I can go back to work. If they're the same, we'll wait three years and try again." God will not be mocked; He who opens and closes the womb will not take orders from yuppie brides.

One thing we miss in our technological age is this wisdom: life is a profound mystery. Almost daily I find myself staring at one of my children, and wondering, "How did this happen? Once this person, the object of my love, was not; and now there will never again be a time when he will not be." There was a point in time when my children began, but there will be no time when they end.

It did not happen because of chemical reactions—though God may have used them. It did not happen because of the marital act—though God may have used that. It happened because God made it happen. No pill, no barrier, not even abstinence can close a womb that God has willed open. And no charts, no Petri dishes, no thermometers can open a womb that God has willed closed.

Children are the most tangible, tactile evidence of the work of God that we will ever see on this green earth. They are a constant reminder of our own weakness, our own dependence, because we are His children. And they are a constant reminder of His great strength, His power, His authority, and His grace. We are not due the blessings He sends; but we are called to worship and thank Him for sending them, to acknowledge the Giver, and we are neither to refuse His gifts nor to wrench them from His hand.

We are His children. We are not the masters of all we survey; rather we are servants of the Master, who made and controls all that He surveys, whether it is a smoothly running computer or a cranky Macintosh, whether it is a closed or a fruitful womb. Let us honor Him by staying out of His way, by acknowledging His absolute authority and trusting Him to do that which honors Him and sanctifies us.

Perhaps one sign that we are in a technological age is that we tend to equate technology with machines. But technology is not just about machines. Technology includes in its range of meaning the entire idea of *techniques*. Human technology need not refer to mechanical pacemakers, but instead can refer to the systems by which we bring about changes in humans. Both a ten-ton bottle-capping machine and an insightful question are tools; one keeps a bottle of soda from spilling and going flat on the way to market, while the other, one hopes, provides insights toward spiritual growth. The difficulty is when we begin to see our friends, our families and our churches as an assembly line of bottles, in need of the right cap.

Much of the wise criticism that has been made against the church over the last ten to twenty years falls into one of two jeremiads. Sometimes we chasten the church for succumbing to that spirit of the age which we call the therapeutic revolution. Other times we chasten the church for bedding down with a different spirit of the age, the one that we call the managerial revolution. In the former, the church exists to soothe the tender spirits of the congregants, to keep the pop from losing its fizz with a dose of pop-psychology. In the latter the spiritual CEO organizes the troops and motivates them until they become an efficient ministry, until they are turned into—what else?—a well-oiled machine.

These two models for the church share two things in common: they are both utterly unbiblical; and they are both technologically minded. They see the church and its members as products we must manipulate to bring about a desired end.

The Bible never describes the church in these technological terms. Never is the church called that which guides the soul toward health, nor that which provides the greatest efficiency for the building of the kingdom. The Bible has all sorts of analogies for the church, none of them technological; instead each of them is organic.

The church is not a set of gears and levers, a clockwork orange; rather it is a set of limbs and appendages, or, as Paul describes it in I Corinthians, a body. Of course that might not steer us completely clear of our problem. We're so technological that we have come even to think of God's great gift of our own bodies as yet another machine to be tweaked to maximize efficiency. We see our parts as parts, and miss the holiness of the whole.

Paul has another image for us, however, that is hard to reduce to something made down at the machine shop. Paul says that we—the church as a whole—are the bride of Christ. Now, brides are not given to technology. I'm not saying that tools are a man thing and ladies should stand clear; rather I'm saying that when we think bride, we necessarily think in organic and not in machine terms. No one says as the bride walks the aisle, "Mercy, look at the torque she's able to handle with her medial collateral ligaments." No one says to the bride, "You know, that veil of yours is not ergonomically designed for the giving of a kiss. Why not leave it off?" No one brings a stopwatch to measure the bride's time in getting up the aisle. A bride is not meant to be efficient but to be beautiful.

We will never read a church bulletin that states, "First Community Church By the Freeway's purpose is to look really, really nice for Jesus." Or, "Our first priority here at Our Lady of the Perpetual Committee Non-Denominational International Family Center is to clean ourselves up good for the wedding day." Yet that is precisely the business of the church and the source of its health.

I'm not suggesting that we shouldn't be working to proclaim

the good news, or that we must cease and desist from visiting the sick. I'm not saying we can never have a church picnic for the sake of fellowship or never deliver turkeys to the poor. Instead, I'm saying we do these things—and all that we do—in order to make us more beautiful as a bride. We are not a machine that needs to be tuned but a bride that needs to be beautified. That's not only what the Groom has called us to do but what He is doing in us.

That's not all, though. Brides do far more—though never less—than look their best. We are indeed a trophy to our Lord, but we are more. Brides have other callings as well, the first of which is to love and to honor the Groom.

The problem with machines is that they lack heart, something the church must cultivate. We are to grow in our love of Christ, to love Him more each day—not with our gears and our levers, but with our hearts and souls, minds and strengths. That is why we study Him and His Word, and meet Him at His table. That is why our preachers preach His glory—that our hearts and minds may be filled with sincere affections.

That we are a bride is a given; we were made for such. And so when we take a technological approach to our calling, we turn our Groom into a machine. He is not a machine. He is not a tool by which, if we punch in the right code, we can have happy, successful, well-ordered lives. He is not a means—which is all tools are—to some other end. Instead our Groom is the end. He is our delight and our joy, not because of what He has done, because of what He now does, or because of what He will do, but because of what He is.

He will succeed. Because our Groom is altogether sovereign in authority and in power, He will get us to see what He has already told us: we are His spotless bride. And when we see it, maybe then we will be spotless, besmirched with neither grease nor sin.

CHAPTER 7

Humility

&

He has shown you, O man,
what is good; and what does the LORD
require of you but to do justly,
to love mercy, and to walk humbly
with your God?

&

Micah 6:8

Recently I had dinner with a few local pastors. One of them raised one of those inevitable conundrums that tend to confront ministers of the cloth. We all took our turn trying to untie the Gordian knot, until the final pastor gave the most wisdom, saying: "That's one of those questions that I respond to with, 'Sin complicates things.'"

Indeed it does. Perhaps the only things worse than the complications that finds their way into our lives through sin are the further complications that comes when we forget about sin. It's bad enough walking through a pasture full of land mines without doing so in ignorance.

Such is true not only in terms of our individual lives but corporately as well. The whole western world began its long descent into death when it first asserted that it was reborn, during the Renaissance and its extension, the Enlightenment. The Enlightenment is a complex of ideas taken from nearly all branches of inquiry. As an epistemology it held that man could know all that he needs to know without the crutch of revelation from God. As a theology it was deistic, affirming that God had created a mechanistic world, wound it up and went out for a walk, never to return. As an anthropology it held that man is fundamentally good. Add them all together and you get Enlightenment optimism, the idea that with the right application of brains and brawn we'll make our way back to the garden. We have the technology; we can rebuild us. And so they tried.

They tried in France, crowning the goddess Reason and uncrowning untold thousands through the ministrations of Madame Guillotine. They tried as revolution continued to spread across Europe and colonialism spread across the Southern Hemisphere in the nineteenth century. And all along the way, as sin continued to complicate things, we were told to practice patience, to try harder, to keep the faith. If the neighbors don't cooperate with your utopian vision, just annex them.

Along came the twentieth century. We began it with the world's First World War. The visionaries, while still refusing to recognize sin, did recognize that war tended to delay the arrival of paradise. So they decided to outlaw war, creating the League of Nations and giving the Germans a positively overpowering dose of negative reinforcement with the Treaty of Versailles.

Meanwhile, the financial Frankensteins were being attacked by the monster of their own creation as the Federal Reserve System sucked the whole world into a depression. Then there was the second Great War, the holocaust, Stalin's gulags and—the crowning achievement of man's unaided reason—the utter destruction of Dresden, Nagasaki, and Hiroshima. Enlightenment optimism has gone up in the smoke of mushroom clouds. Paradise remains lost.

There are, of course, still some old enlightenment-modernist dinosaurs out roaming the land. They keep promising that the garden is just around the corner. But nobody is paying them any attention. We have learned from our hubris. We will not build another Babel, nor don the wings of Icarus again. Instead we'll remain earthbound and babble to ourselves.

The reaction to this failure was the embracing of failure, to create not a paradise but a safe place to stay by confessing our utter ignorance and denying that we are good. This is the postmodern way, in which we know that we can know nothing and that *good* and *bad* aren't even meaningful concepts. We cannot communicate among ourselves, because each of us assigns his own meanings to words. We cannot love our brother because, being unable to walk a mile in his moccasins, we cannot know him.

Where is the church in all this? During the glory days of the Enlightenment, the church was there cheering it on, doing its part to impart the ethic of Jesus the moral teacher. In the aftermath we are with the dinosaurs, still believing that if we could but get enough Republicans in office, or enough men into football stadiums, or enough true believers barking in the aisles in Toronto, at that point we'd have what we need for paradise.

It is the same pride. Equipped with Freud and the Bible

we will make people whole. Equipped with the Bible and the right marketing strategy we will win the lost and save America. Equipped with enough delegates we will get prayer back in our schools, and then we will have won. Equipped with a big enough coalition the gates of Disney will not prevail against us. We have maintained the fundamental idea—that we can create a paradise—but have chosen slightly different tools. Like the Enlightenment gurus, we have forgotten about sin.

The church remembers sin, but believes that it's *out there*. Sin is not *out there* but *in here*. Were we able to recreate paradise, all we'd accomplish is another fall; the second we step into the garden it contains weeds. We carry sin around with us, wherever we go.

Nevertheless, we do have a grand utopian scheme. The problem with Enlightenment optimism is not its optimism, but the blindness and foolishness of an optimism that looks for perfection in all the wrong places. We will create paradise on earth not because we are basically good or because we can discover all that we need to know on our own; we will create paradise on earth because Jesus has revealed all that we need to know, and because He is not only basically good but only and altogether good. Because of Jesus we reject the prideful utopianism of the modernists; because of Jesus we reject the humiliated despair of the post-modernists.

To put it another way, we are humble about ourselves, yet we boast in Christ. Humility was a virtue badly needed during the Enlightenment. And in another sense we need it now as well. The complete loss of hope in knowledge that drives post-modernism is rooted in a claim of omniscience. The complete loss of hope in the power to change things is rooted in a claim of omnipotence. In modernism we thought that we could be like God and order the universe to our own whims; in postmodernism we thought that we could be like God and create reality in the unreachable recesses of our own minds. First we thought we could bend reality; when reality wouldn't cooperate, we decided we'd be better off creating our own reality, one with its own set of rules.

In both systems, sin corrupts. We seek to restructure or to recreate reality for our own pleasure and our own glory. God, however, has no such limitations. He created for His own pleasure and for His own glory, which is the appropriate thing for God to do. And now His Son is recreating, restructuring reality to overcome sin, and again rightly doing so for His own glory. And He starts with us. He remakes us into His image. We are the first of His utopian projects, ones that He completes one by one at our deaths. But it does not end until all things are in subjection to Him, until everything but Gehenna is paradise.

Humility teaches us that we will fail, and that He will not. Humility teaches us that paradise is absent because of our sin. Humility teaches us not only that we are imperfect but that we are wretched. Even in the church we at times forget the depth of our sin, both individually and corporately. We get impatient for the end and so fail to see how far away we are. We think we're pretty good, and that we live in a pretty good place; that's why we think all it will take is more rallies, or more 'conservatives' in office. Evangelical utopianism affirms with its lips that we are sinners, but affirms with its actions that we're not that bad, that we're almost there.

We have rightly rejected Enlightenment epistemology. We have rightly—though not sufficiently—rejected Enlightenment anthropology. We have rightly held onto Enlightenment optimism; but we have wrongly held onto Enlightenment strategy for building paradise. We maintain essential self-sufficiency— though we concede it's a good thing to pray.

And we maintain a lack of humility over how far we have to go, and continue to think in terms of grand schemes. We need to seize power, and then we'll be able to get something done. We need flash and visibility; we need to seize the controls of pop culture. We'll take over Harvard, NBC, MGM, CNN and ESPN, and then it's all over but the crying for the bad guys.

And what happens when we succeed? Because we forget our sin, we fail. When our pop singers cross over into the rest of the world—surprise—they become just like the rest of the world. When our favored political sons win office, they find they want to keep it, and so sell their souls for it. Heck, we *built* Harvard, Yale and Princeton—and look where they are now.

We need humility, to have a better understanding of our own sin and how far we have to go. We need to set right our own garden before we go out into the jungle. In short, our goal should not be to seize the power centers but to be faithful in the real, biblical power centers—our homes and in our churches. When Jesus gets our house in order, then He will move on into the world. To think otherwise is to get way ahead of ourselves.

What we need to do is to get back to the garden. The garden we are called to now is not Eden but our own homes, our own families, our own communities. We need to think small before we get big thoughts. That's why we at the Highlands Study Center do things the odd way we do them.

You will never receive a come-on from Draught Horse Press arguing that our work is the linchpin of the kingdom, that if you get behind us we'll do so much for the kingdom that we'll live on in church history. We're not going like David to fight the Goliath of Washington or New York or Hollywood; instead we're going like David out into the pasture, to tend a few sheep. We're not going to save the American family from the forces of evil. We're going to try, by the grace of our King, to save our own families from the forces of evil, and to encourage you to do the same.

We're doing more for the kingdom when we take it upon ourselves to teach our children than anything we could do to lobby some school board to allow creationism to be taught at the government school. We need to begin our work in the building of the kingdom by humbly taking on the first task Jesus has given us—to obey Him. If He wants to give us political power and to make us culture brokers, He'll do it in His time, in His way.

And He won't do it by building assorted coalitions with idolaters who, like us, don't like a lot of cuss words in our movies.

That's what it means to live simple, separate and deliberate lives. We at the Center are simple in part because we don't come with a grand scheme; instead we quietly encourage others to think and act simply, separately and deliberately. We teach whoever will listen who God is, what man is, and how they relate; we teach people the Word of God, face to face, a few people at a time. We are separate because we want to get the world out of our lives before we start bringing our lives to the world. We are deliberate because we question the assumptions—including the assumption that you have to think big to have a big impact—and because we have thought of our limitations.

We are humble about ourselves, but bold about the crown rights of King Jesus. We do it not as retreatists but for the glory of God and for the building of His kingdom. We tend our garden not out of indifference to the jungle, but so that we might be something set apart, so that the jungle might long for the peace, the beauty, the simplicity that is ours in Christ, the Lord of the Garden.

We live in an age of uncertainty; we are ignorant of our past and fearful of our future. And in the here and now—well, we just don't know. The one thing we're sure of is that we're not sure at all. That is a part of the folly of postmodernism. The self-referential nature of its epistemology is immediately, obviously, and devastatingly absurd. It affirms the truth that there is no truth; it says you are false if you affirm there is a false. But the contradictions do not stop there. It is not only epistemological nonsense, it is also moral nonsense.

As postmodernism crept into our culture it came in the thoughts and works of a ragtag band of mourning Jeremiahs. Sartre wept over the death of truth, as did his compatriot Camus. Kierkegaard may have been the melancholy Dane but Nietzsche was not a man you wanted to invite to a party. Theirs was no giddy celebration of emancipation but a doleful realization that we are but strangers in a hostilely indifferent universe.

It's ironic that the younger generation, those who find the lightness of being rather bearable, in some ways are more consistent than their fathers. Consider: why would one mourn to discover that there is no truth? One cannot mourn unless one presupposes that it is true that truth has value. If nothing is true, it's not true that truth has value. And so nothing is lost. And so there should be no mourning. Perhaps they have learned the lesson—though we can't say that it is true that it is false to think that it is sad that there is no truth—if in fact there is no truth.

The younger generation, however, has its own version of the same inconsistency. They not only don't mourn the loss of truth, they attack as evil those few of us left who affirm that there is truth. One of the supposed great advantages of relativism is what it can do for peace. If Roman Catholicism can be true for you, and Protestantism true for me, but neither can *really* be true— then why all the fighting in occupied Ireland? If Judaism has no claim on the Muslim, and Islam none on the Jew, we need no more summits at Camp David. The problem is solved; if we will just agree to disagree, or agree to agree that it is true that none of what we affirm is true, then peace will descend like the dew.

Some of us don't agree. We affirm that Jesus is Lord, over those who in His grace recognize it, and those who do not; we affirm that there is true truth, and that relativism is a lie. And so we are attacked.

Sometimes we are attacked lawlessly, as in Waco or in Nazi Germany. Sometimes we are attacked through the law, as in the silencing of abortion protesters. (Of course, war does break out every time your reality clashes with mine. To me, it's fine for me to take what you own; to you, perhaps not. And so the shooting starts.) But so far—and believe me, this is changing—we are merely attacked socially. That is, we are called names. And tops on the list is *arrogant*.

That is what we are called, whoever the 'we' is that affirms objective, knowable reality. "Who do we think we are? Do we think we have a corner on the truth? Who are we to say what's true and what's false? Where is our humility? We always think we're right!"

The pimps of tolerance won't tolerate us walking on their street corner; it's bad for business. And sadly, many of us are just relativists enough that we let this nonsense get to us. We bend and scrape, and plead, and make sure we let everyone know that some of our best friends are relativists. In doing this we miss the simple hypocrisy of their judgment. We miss the opportunity to respond, "Are you saying it is objectively true that I should never say that something is objectively true? Are you saying it is wrong for me to say that anything is wrong?"

But we also miss the most astounding hypocrisy of all, that they think that they have mastered humility and that we have the arrogance problem. Ask them which is more arrogant: I say that there is an objective reality outside of myself. I did not make it, I do not control it, I cannot comprehend it in its totality; but I can—and you can—know something about it that is real and true. Or: I say that I create all reality. Whatever is, is because I believe it to be so; and neither you, nor some god, nor anyone else can change the reality that I have constructed in my own head. To me sodomy is fine, and as such it can never be judged.

Relativism is not rooted in epistemological humility but in the very ontological pride with which the serpent tempted Eve. Bite into relativism and you shall be as God, creating reality, morality, all that is. Our view in turn turns on the conviction that the God who made us also made all things, and that He has revealed some things to us so that we can know them. We are the subjects of reality, not its master.

Relativism is not humility; it is humiliating. It is the non-system of non-sense that falls of its own weight before it can take a step. All the moral posturing is just that—the faux posture of those slouching toward Gehenna.

We are indeed called to be humble, to recognize that there but for the grace of God go all of us. But we must never be humble about God, and about His revelation of Himself. We must never confuse our own wishes with His reality—especially when it comes to Him, when we write off His attributes by speaking of "God-to-me". He is what He is; that's His name. And we are His creatures, who must believe and affirm all that He teaches.

While it is true that the road to hell is paved with good intentions, there's a difference between ambling down that road in ignorance and being forced to march down that road. It is worse to be wicked than ignorant.

Perhaps one thing that separates my railing against the state from the mere grumbling of others is my belief that the state is not merely dumb but wicked. I don't believe that the state operates with the best of intentions, while unfortunately failing to understand the basic tenets of the Constitution or of common sense. The state knows what it's doing.

And it does what it does out of the same sin by which the first creature fell—pride. The state did not become a leviathan by accident; it became one because it wants to be God.

Adam and Eve were called to be God's vice-regents, to rule for Him. They chose instead to seek to rule instead of Him. They stepped outside their bounds because they wanted a bigger job.

Like Adam and Eve, the state was given a task. The state has been given the sword and charged by God with the task of punishing evildoers. Which evildoers? Certainly not all of them. When my son Campbell fails to clean his room as I command him, it is not a legitimate function of the state to discipline him; that's daddy's job. When I start teaching heresy from the pulpit, we are not to call the sheriff but the session. The state oversteps its bounds when it determines that it must punish each and every wrongdoer.

But it gets much worse. The state today not only punishes wrongdoers outside its jurisdiction, but it engages in all manner of activities that have little or nothing to do with punishment. Even if the state won't throw me in the slammer for not eating my veggies, it does buy airtime on the radio and television telling me over and over how many servings the scientists they've hired think I should have. Even if they don't put me in the stocks for failing to prepare for my old age, they do take my money from me every month, use it to take care of other older folks, and promise they'll tax my children to take care of me when I'm old. There is no sword here—save that these are all paid for by taxes taken by force—but there is an attempt to control all that I do.

The state believes it has the power and wisdom to build a perfect world; that's why there is a government school system. The function of the government schools from the start was not to educate the people but to control them, to indoctrinate them in the religion of the state. If the state loves the spotted owls, they must teach the kids to love the spotted owls. If the state wants us to embrace sodomy, then they must train our kids in diversity. If the state believes that Jesus Christ is a matter of indifference to the pursuit of truth—well, then, we just won't mention Him. The final arbiter of all questions of truth will be the state.

A humble state knows not only its calling but also the One who called it. A humble state is one with the wisdom to leave on the shackles of those limitations of the calling that God has placed on it, and to kiss the Son, lest He become angry (Psalm 2). It stays within its appointed boundaries and operates as a minister of God, fulfilling its particular calling.

A humble state knows it can't keep people from smoking or drinking or eating too much. It can't make sure we all get enough exercise. It can't find a cure for AIDS. It can't feel our pain, make us wise, or make us godly. It can't make sure that no one thinks in terms of racial stereotypes. It can't make sure daddies love their children. It can't provide babysitting for single moms—and even if it could, it can't pay for it without taking money out of the pockets of single moms. It can't help young families buy their first home. It can't manipulate interest rates or the money supply to guarantee perpetual growth.

As the next election season reaches its peak, see if there are any humble men running for the office of leader of the purportedly free world. We ought to have an overpowering distrust toward anyone who wants the power to remake the world according to his own wisdom. We ought to know that we cannot support any man who doesn't say first, "I will only punish wrongdoers," and second, "If the Constitution doesn't list it as our job, we're just not going to do it." We need a man with the humility to recognize that when Lord Acton said, "Power corrupts, and absolute power corrupts absolutely," that Lord Acton was talking to *him*. We need a man who will kiss the Son, and do it boldly.

Perhaps more important is that we also have the humility to know our own place. We need to recognize that the state does not exist to make our life more comfortable. We share in the wickedness when we ask the state to step beyond its calling, when we ask it to feed us in our old age, to feed the widows in our midst, to help us go to college, to teach our children, to make sure our mutual fund does not tumble too far. We too want to be like God, believing that the cattle on a thousand hills belong to us rather than acknowledging that they are under the stewardship of our neighbors.

But we are not a humble people. Until we repent, we will be just another faction clamoring for dollars, to enact our own vision of political utopia. Until we are humbled, we will only continue to be humiliated.

C<small>HAPTER</small>

Holy Days

&

This is the day the LORD has made;
we will rejoice and be glad in it.

G

Psalm 118:24

race is amazing. The word itself amazes, fitting so many shades of meaning into such a tiny word. We use the word to describe a sense of gentility, as we would speak of the grace found in a fine southern gentle lady. We use the word to describe that time period that falls between when our bills are due and when those we owe start to call us names. We use the word to describe the common ritual—and I use the term ritual not in any pejorative sense—which we go through before we eat our meals.

And then of course there is the most amazing grace of all: the showering of God's favor upon His children who deserve nothing of the sort. Here the word falls infinitely short of being able to contain the thing signified.

It is possible, however, that its very greatness is its very weakness. Because grace means so much it can and often does come to mean so little. Whether we are speaking of God's particular grace, or His common grace, too often it seems too common. We become like fish in water, too immersed to notice that it is all around us. We've grown accustomed to His grace, and so take it and Him for granted.

A table grace exists in part to help alleviate the problem. We are presented with bounty. We think it got there because of all our hard work, or because of the booming economy, or, more likely, just because it is supposed to be there; it's there every day, after all. But we stop, and remember that none of the above is so. We remember that the food is there because God has graciously provided it for us.

And once a year we have a particularly large feast, not so the men can watch a great deal of football but to remember that God has been gracious to us throughout the year. But even this liturgy can become rote to us. We gather together, and forget what we are gathered for. We're too busy worrying about basting the turkey and cooking the yams that our holy day, our celebration of the Lord's provision, becomes just another job, another occasion to grumble about all the work we do.

We don't come to this feast as our fathers did. We are not running out of last year's provision, scraping the bottom of the barrel and waiting and hoping that the crop will ripen and that it will be full. Instead we come to this feast full from the meal we ate just a few hours before. We are provided for richly, day in and day out, and so we have a famine of gratitude for the grace.

The Scripture tells us that this failure of gratitude is at the heart of the sins of men. Paul, in addressing the church at Rome, says of the unregenerate: "For though they knew God, they neither glorified Him as God nor gave thanks to Him" (Romans 1:21). We, however, are regenerate; we should therefore be marked as a people consumed with worship, and with gratitude. But our old man is still kicking, and so gratitude is still a problem.

That's why God has given us liturgies, as an aid to remembering. Whether it is the feast of weeks in the old covenant or the weekly feast in the new covenant, we are to gather together to give thanks. We are to remember and to recite together the great deeds of God in our lives, and in the lives of our fathers. We are to take the time to be satisfied in Him and in His provision. That we turn these memory aids into an excuse for forgetting, that we take for granted not only the grace but the gracious reminder of the grace is no excuse to forget the reminder. We don't avoid giving thanks lest the ritual become too familiar; rather, lest the grace become too familiar, we take the time for the ritual.

We must give thanks daily. We must recognize that each day is a gift from God. That we are not suffering His eternal wrath, which is what we daily deserve, ought to set our hearts to singing. That we are alive ought to surprise us. That we are not only alive but blessed in countless ways ought to astonish us.

"This is the day that the Lord hath made; let us rejoice and be glad in it" the Psalmist declares to the congregation. Every day is a holy day because it was made by a holy God. Our response must be as follows: to follow our duty and to rejoice in it. The returning of thanks is not to be a chore to us, but a joyous cause for celebration.

About ten years ago an economist named Paul Zane Pilzer wrote a best-selling book titled *Unlimited Wealth*. This was not the typical gloom that comes from the pens of professors in what has been called the dismal science; Pilzer was rather optimistic about our economic future—which, I believe, was rather foolish. But I was reminded of something terribly important while reading the book. While there certainly is such a thing as absolute poverty, most of what we experience is merely relative poverty.

Absolute poverty is that which causes starvation; relative poverty merely causes relative privation. Pilzer explained that much of the gloom and doom that has come from the economists is not really the result of a stagnant economy but the result of a culture in which our desires have outpaced our ability to meet them. That is, we feel poor not because we are poor but because we're not as rich as we would like to be. Because we can imagine having more, we think we're suffering for not having it.

Pilzer illustrated the point with homes. Everyone knows how horrible it is that young couples have such a hard time purchasing their first home; this is supposed to be a sign that something is wrong with the economy. What is left out of the equation is what kind of home young homebuyers are typically trying to buy. The average home today is twice the size of the average home just fifty years ago. When the last generation did manage to buy a home, they filled it with matchstick furniture; we take the plastic down to Ethan Allan and lug home the debt on our backs. The average home fifty years ago had one television, if any; today the average is closer to three than two. It's not the economy, stupid—it's our acquisitiveness. We want more, and we want it now.

Such not only fails to cultivate a grateful heart, but it creates resentful hearts. We tell ourselves we're not greedy, we just want what's "normal." And normal is defined as the next step up, wherever we are on the economic scale.

Are we amazed that most of us, every day, sometimes twice a day, can take a nice warm shower, without giving a thought to the cost? I remember being allowed to run through the house when I was a boy, but only when it was that most special of occasions—when someone was calling long distance and I had to fetch a parent. Now we ask the caller from across the country to hang on a second while we finish vacuuming the rug. And when the pinch comes at the end of the month we grumble to our spouse—or worse, to God.

The good news is that we can—indeed we must—turn this all upside down. God is not commanding us to rejoice in our want but to rejoice in His bountiful provision. If we really understand what is due to us, how can we do anything but celebrate in the presence of such bounty? It is true of our economic lives, our spiritual lives, all of our lives. Can I imagine having more? Of course I can. Can I imagine being owed more? Not on your life. Even in the midst of absolute poverty, if our stomachs are swelled not from the bounty but from the want, we have Jesus. This is the day that the Lord hath made; let us rejoice and be glad in it.

That's part of what it means to live a simple life. It doesn't mean giving up the finer things in life; in fact, it means learning to recognize the finer things in life. Our problem, as C.S. Lewis has argued, is not that we are too hard to satisfy but that we are too easy to satisfy; we'd rather play in the gutter than come to the Master's feast. It doesn't mean treating the bounty of God as if it were some sort of infectious disease. This is the day that the Lord hath made; let us rejoice and be glad in it.

I'm not arguing that it is bad to have things, even nice things; I am saying that our expectations are to be simple. Our lives are not set on getting the newest and greatest thing. Our eyes are not set on the blessings of our neighbors, nor our teeth set on edge with envy. This is the day that the Lord hath made; let us rejoice and be glad in it.

When we live our days as the holy days that they are, then we will live our days in a holy way—set apart, distinct, and separate. That means our priorities are not the world's priorities. It means that while the world is despairing over its perceived wants, we are rejoicing in our actual blessings. It means that we measure our blessings on the Almighty's scales. It means that we delight in the truth that our cup runneth over, even when we are eating beans again. We are not like them. We have been born again. We are Kings and Queens. We have Jesus. This is the day that the Lord hath made; let us rejoice and be glad in it.

We ought to be deliberate, not just in our doing but in our thinking. We must recognize that our perceptions of the good life—of normalcy, of prosperity—are to come not from the television but from the Word of God. We should refuse the lie that says the good life is measured by the horsepower in our car and the limit on our credit card. These are the very lies of the devil that rob us of our joy and turn our hearts from gratitude; as such, they are the very ideas with which we are at war. This is the day that the Lord hath made; let us rejoice and be glad in it.

We do not go about our daily labors as the world does, either to acquire the cash to buy the happiness or to acquire the cash to pay down the debt we acquired when we last tried to buy happiness. We are not debt slaves, but neither are we our own. We have been bought with a price, and so drafted into the Lord's army. Our labors are our calling to exercise dominion over God's creation as servants of the King of Kings. We labor, wherever we labor, for the glory of God and the building of His kingdom. Isn't that cause to rejoice? Our labor has meaning, eternal meaning. We have waiting for us an eternal reward that is greater than our capacity to even imagine. And in the meantime we have families and friends and pleasures and delights and comforts. This is the day that the Lord has made; let us rejoice and be glad in it.

When we recognize that all our days are holy days, then we daily feast before the Lord. Resentment, disappointment, frustration, envy—all are banished from this feast. God has been gracious, and He always will be gracious; we move through our lives from grace to grace, from blessing to blessing. This is the day that the Lord hath made; let us rejoice and be glad in it.

And there is still more. When we forget once more to give thanks, when we forget once more to rejoice before the Lord, when we forget once more His amazing grace—amazingly, He will forgive. His grace covers even our forgetting of His grace, as in Christ He forgets our forgetfulness. If you are despairing instead of rejoicing, do not despair—repent, and rejoice. Thank Him for His grace in reminding you of His grace. Don't wait. Don't consider it. Do it now, because this is the day that the Lord hath made; let us rejoice and be glad in it.

Someone once told me of a fairly large family travelling on a long trip. They were flying by air, and the mother had cut a deal with their children: she explained that if the children were peaceful, obedient, and quiet while on the plane, then she would buy them ice cream once they landed on the ground. Through the flight the children were so angelic that one would have thought they weren't simply visiting the heavens but living there. Others on the long flight took the trouble of speaking to the parents, praising their children for their outstanding behavior. Once in the terminal however, the angels fell quickly, screaming and whining: "Where's my ice cream? Gimme my ice cream!" Bribes can effectively—though temporarily—mask a rebellious heart, but they won't change one.

Such, however, need not mean that we will never reward our children for a job well done. We are falling off the other side of the bicycle if, after having successfully learning how to ride a bicycle, our children are congratulated with a yawn. They are rather excited, and so should we be excited.

We ought to celebrate achievement in our homes and in our home schools, and do it often. These celebrations, of course, should not be for show. Too often our children's parties devolve into Martha Stewart imitation contests, with each mother trying to outdo the other. You should not be bragging about your child, nor your ability to entertain with flair. Celebrations certainly can be large, if the occasion warrants it, but they can also be small.

When, for instance, our oldest daughter Darby successfully mastered a set of fifty catechism questions written for very small children, we loaded up the children and headed off for hamburgers and ice cream; it was cheap, easy, and a delight to Darby. We did the same when our son Campbell reached the same milestone. Smaller still, when Campbell read his first real book, I fetched a candy bar for him. In both instances we were celebrating an achievement, not in the context of a contest but in the context of learning.

I have had the privilege of attending three different celebrations of high school graduation since we moved to Virginia, all three for young people who had completed their home school studies. None of these were desperate attempts to recreate the whole high school graduation experience lest the children feel somehow left out; they were not the final folly of doing school at home. These were bigger celebrations in the context of a greater achievement—these godly young scholars had all excelled, and fulfilled the promises in Proverbs that godly seed are an honor to their parents. All three occasions were opportunities for parents to communicate to their children how pleased they were, not only with their studies but with their characters.

And don't leave yourselves out of the picture. We continue to labor and we continue to learn. And so we should continue to celebrate our accomplishments. In our spare refrigerator we have a bottle of champagne; it is waiting, not for anything in particular, but for an appropriate time of celebration. Our joy will not be put on hold while we run down to the store. It's ready, and so are we, for the right time.

In all of these instances we are trying to remember landmarks. To stop and celebrate these events is not at all unlike the command of Joshua to mark the spot with stones where the children of Israel crossed over the Jordan river and into the land long promised. We are not violating the regulative principle of worship; we are remembering the blessings of God in our own lives, just as our fathers did before us.

Remembering God's grace is, of course, a critical part of the equation. We not only have nothing that God has not given us, we have done nothing that He has not first brought to pass. He is the one manifesting His glory as our children grow to be more like Jesus. He is the one working in them both to do and to will His good pleasure. Our celebrations of achievement, whether large or small, are remembrances of the grace of God. Indeed, *all* of our celebrations must be remembrances of the grace of God.

If we are stingy in our praise of our children, we are probably also stingy in our praise of their heavenly Father. That we begin with high expectations is no reason not to be excited when those expectations are met or exceeded. That we rejoice in their accomplishments is not to suggest that we expect little from them. To not rejoice is to be ungrateful. If we delight in them, we will likewise delight in the One who gave them to us.

Perhaps homeschooling parents are reluctant to celebrate because of those remaining fears that we don't really know what we're doing; we can't celebrate step A because we're still not sure we'll get to step B. All that means is that we have more learning—and unlearning—to do. We should forget all the dire warnings of the naysayers, remember the promises of God and enter into our task confident in our children, and confident in ourselves, all because we are confident in the grace of God.

Don't be a sourpuss. Don't be afraid to rejoice. God is good, and He is good to us, and to our children. Feast in His presence, and give thanks.

Every religion has its meta-narrative. *Meta-narrative* is a fancy, obfuscating word for *story*, a story that puts one's fundamental concerns and beliefs into context. As

Christians our meta-narrative is a simple one: creation, fall, and re-creation.

Meta-narratives also put holy days into context. Every religion, in its story, includes events of great significance, and those great events are remembered and celebrated. So every religion has its holy days. So does the religion of the state.

Our national meta-narrative, of course, is not grounded in any sort of inerrant document, and as such it tends to drift over time. Our parents were regaled with stories of the heroics of the founding fathers. They recited in school that poem about Paul Revere's ride. They put on school plays recreating the crossing of the Delaware. And they celebrated as a holy day the anniversary of Washington's birth.

Such has fallen out of favor of late, principally because Washington loved freedom and considered the British rule—although benign compared with what we suffer under today—to be utterly despotic. Now we in America have President's Day instead, when presumably we celebrate Clinton and Johnson—Andrew, who was also impeached—and every other scoundrel that made it to the White House. Independence Day is still celebrated, but with all the fireworks and cookouts one would be hard pressed to remember why.

As the size of the state grew, so did the number of days which it laid claim to. At the acme of the labor movement in this country we were treated to another high holy day—Labor Day. Here we are told to celebrate labor, to toss one back in honor of the lunch bucket crowd. But as we have, with the advent of internationalism, exported our labor across the globe, we have again forgotten what all the hub-bub was about, and so we celebrate a Monday off.

We have two separate holy days to celebrate our successes on assorted battlefields around the globe, Memorial Day and Veterans Day. Here we honor the dead and the living for dying and fighting in defense of—of—well, that's where it gets a little complicated. And so again we forget.

Our narrative has now ceased to celebrate what we are supposed to be as Americans. We are united only in that we are committed together to be less than united. Multiculturalism rules the day, and so we have begun to divvy up the remaining days among the faithful unfaithful.

On Columbus Day we no longer celebrate the discovery of the New World. We do not want to encourage our young to become rapacious, disease-carrying oppressors of noble savages. So instead we have turned it into an Italian Saint Patrick's Day.

The most heinous of all, however, is the newest of holy days in the state religion—Martin Luther King Day. I have a dream that a day will come when we as a nation will judge our heroes by the content of their character and not the color of their skin. That day is not here yet. You know you're involved in a rather lame religion when one of your holy days celebrates the life of an unrepentant, plagiarizing womanizer. Come to think of it, why not just merge it with President's Day?

While such has not yet reached federal status, rest assured that Pink Triangle day is coming, a federal holy day to celebrate sodomy. Our politicos already honor the local celebrations with their presence; it is but a short step for all of us to have a day off to enjoy the spectacle of queers on parade. Be sure to tell your kids not to take the candy.

My point is not principally the nature of these holy days, the things we're called to celebrate, but to further make the case that we have indeed fallen deeply into statism. Statism is not merely the growth of the power of the state; it is a religion in which the state is worshipped. The state becomes as god. They are the ones who determine what and when we will treat as sacred. We get our fill of liturgical remembrance at the barbecue pit and drink the sacred wine of cold Bud. Our days are now ordered by those who order us about day by day.

I'm not suggesting that we ought not to remember the sacrifices or the wisdom of the founding fathers; I am suggesting that this same wisdom would be arguing as I am arguing, that we have too much of the state in our lives. I'm not suggesting that we ought not to remember the dead and the living who have fought in wars under honorable flags; I am suggesting that to do so we have to do the messy work of determining which of those flags flew—and they were few—honorably. We can still honor valorous soldiers, even if that valor was used in the service of empire, as in all our recent wars. But we cannot honor the state for building empire.

What we need to do is check what we're celebrating and who is throwing the bash before we join the party. We need to have our Daytimers booked up with things worth celebrating. We are citizens of heaven, and so should work from heaven's calendar.

We need to honor our martyrs before we honor American dead, those who died for an eternal reality rather than a political abstraction. We need to remember heroes like Luther, Calvin and Knox, who brought us the truth, before we get all misty-eyed over of dead politicians who spoke with forked tongues. We need to rejoice in the true Liberator who made us one in Him before we rejoice over that liberation 'theologian' who has made us divided.

We have a meta-narrative worth re-telling and worth celebrating. What's better still, our story is grounded in history. Our legends are true. Our heroes are heroic. But we're too busy cheering on the state to notice. We are not worthy of our fathers in the faith, and so we are left with the god we have earned.

CHAPTER 9

The Acts
of the Apostles

℘

*But you shall receive power when
the Holy Spirit has come upon you;
and you shall be witnesses to Me
in Jerusalem, and in all Judea
and Samaria, and to the end
of the earth*

☙

Acts 1:8

"You shall be My witnesses." The Bible often brings together what we want to keep apart. We want to believe that either one thing is like another, or that it ought to be like another. The truth is that, here and elsewhere, it is both.

When Paul makes a comparison between the love of a husband for a wife and the love of Christ for His church, he says not only that we as husbands are commanded to reflect the love of Christ for His church but also that we necessarily will, either truly or falsely. The connection will be made, and we either show that Christ loves the church or that He does not.

The same is true of this passage, Christ's promise/warning to the disciples in the opening chapter of Acts, which is given just prior to the Ascension. Jesus is speaking face to face with the Apostles for the last time. He is giving them both a charge and a warning. The truth, for good or ill, is that as His appointed messengers, given the authority to speak for Him, they would be His representatives on earth.

And though we do not speak with the same authority as the Apostles, the same is true of the church today. We too are the sent ones; we too are witnesses. When the world asks what Jesus is like, they find their answer in us.

My dear wife Denise and I did a great deal of thinking before we named our son Robert Campbell, making him the fifth generation of R.C.'s. Our intention was to place on him a sense of obligation, a weight of duty because of his name. He must be aware of those men who went before him, wearing the same name.

But the truth is that a few weeks after Denise and I named him, we placed on him a greater burden when he took on the name of Christ through the sacrament of baptism. All you who are relieved that your name isn't R.C. may now start to sweat— that is, if Christ has so marked you, if you bear His name.

This is precisely what the third commandment is all about. It certainly includes an injunction against the frivolous use of the names of God; those pagans on television or in the movies that use His holy name as mere filler will find at the judgment that such was not wise. It may even include a prohibition of salty language—though I tend to doubt it. But the center of the commandment is the injunction against bringing shame or dishonor on the name of God. And we do that every time we sin, if we bear His name.

Taking on the name of Christ means all sorts of wonderful things to us. It most importantly means that He has taken on the punishment of our sin, such that we have peace with the Father. It means that we are credited with His righteousness, such that we, in Him, earn the glory of heaven. It means that though we die, yet will we live, and live forever. It means that we are joint heirs with Christ, that we are and ever more will be kings and queens over the created order. It means that we will see Him as He is, and that we will be like Him.

But it also means we have an obligation; that we are— whether we like it or not—His witnesses. That ought to scare us. It's one thing to tell a lie, another thing altogether to lie about who Jesus is. When I am unkind to a brother I tell the world that Jesus is unkind to His bride. When I impose all sorts of unbiblical law on people I tell the world that His burden is hard and His yoke is heavy. And when I succumb to the allure of the world, when I seek after other gods, I tell the world that Jesus is not a true servant of the Father but an adulterer.

The first century church operated under the very same burden. The only difference is that they didn't have two thousand years of church history behind them. The ministries of mercy that our fathers did around the globe have made it that much easier for us to show to the world who Jesus is. Those in the book of Acts started from scratch; they were the first visible manifestation of the invisible God that they served.

When Stephen was stoned for proclaiming the gospel, then the people knew that this Jesus died that others might have life; and when Stephen beheld the Lord in glory, then they knew that this King who had died and risen was indeed still king. Their task now was to get the word out, through all that they did, about who this Jesus was and is.

On the other hand, perhaps they had some advantages that we lack. When a first-century believer was known to bear the name of Christ, unbelievers did not immediately think of Jim Bakker or Jimmy Swaggert. They didn't have images of folks carrying signs saying, "God hates fags." They didn't have to explain away the crusades.

They carried with them neither any positive momentum nor any unwanted baggage. Yet without these things, in no time at all they developed a reputation, an image—they were known to be rather odd ducks.

I remember sitting on the stage of a Roman amphitheater in Galilee. Our guide who was showing us all around Palestine explained to us that the first century believers would not attend the various games and festivals in the stadia that dotted the land; that doesn't surprise us. But then he explained that at the founding of the church Christians did not steer clear in order to avoid the violence of the gladiator games; nor did they avoid them because some girl in a bikini might walk around between rounds carrying a sign. They didn't go, he said, because they weren't interested. It was no first century boycott, but a true show of indifference.

It was at that point that I vowed to purge my life of the daily intake of SportsCenter and the daily reading of the scores in the paper—in fact, it was then that I gave up on reading the paper. (By the way, lest you think I have broken a vow, I excluded banning the Steelers, not because I thought it was any different, but because it is better not to take a vow than to take one and to break it).

The first century believers didn't go to the games because the games didn't matter. And of course nobody came up with the brilliant strategy of being His witnesses by carrying a sign and wearing a rainbow wig to the game. Neither did the youth dream of becoming successful gladiators so that they might have a chance to thank the man upstairs for the victory.

Purging one's life of spectator sports is, of course, only a small thing. It is, however, a bigger thing than what most of us take to be part of our calling to be set apart. We figure if we smile nicely, maybe if we hum "Amazing Grace" under our breath, maybe if we say, "God bless you" to our business associates over the phone, maybe someone will give us that famous opening for telling them about Jesus, "I've noticed something different about you ..." This is not how we are to be witnesses.

Because our faith touches the whole of our lives, it ought to make the whole of our lives look different. I'm not suggesting that we ought to walk on our hands because the pagans walk on their feet. The more influence we have on the culture by being set apart, the less set apart we will be, because the pagans will begin to act like us. The pagan divorce rate is as high as it is because the Christian divorce rate is as high as it is. If we would start seeing God's children as a blessing, then the pagans would stop killing their children. They follow us, not we them.

And so when we do follow them, we're just the blind leading the blind. We do not separate from them so that they don't see us, but so that they *will* see us. As long as we look like and act like them, there is nothing for them to see. Yet we want to be a lamp under the bushel, a city in the valley, a light obscured by worldliness—lest they think we're strange.

I am suggesting that as we take every thought captive, we will likewise take all our actions captive. Ideas have consequences—in fact, that's what ideas are for. And as we take our actions captive, then we will be accurate witnesses. Jesus was not just one of the guys, and so neither may we be.

I am not suggesting that we ought to be dour. You'll remember that Jesus, though a man well acquainted with sorrows, was called by His enemies a glutton and a winebibber. Consider what happened once during our Feast of Pentecost, an annual party at the Highlands Study Center where we celebrate the return of the Groom in the person of the Spirit. As the crowds poured into our little place here, we began to have a problem with parking. Cars were spilling over into the street. One enterprising neighbor, having spent the early evening home alone with the TV while draining a six-pack, determined that he might get another six-pack out of our dilemma. He slurred an offer to have guests park at his place for only five dollars.

What was the difference between the evening here and the evening there? Was it beer? No, we had beer. Was it his good time and our bad time? More likely the opposite. We were enjoying each other and God's provision. We were gathered in body around our Lord. He was gathered in spirit with distant others watching the same soon-to-be-forgotten television program. While he was trying to make a buck, we were serving one another. We had a grand time, while he was just killing time.

We are like the world in so many ways, ways we are ashamed of. We have had a divorce in our little congregation. But we responded by excommunicating the guilty party and taking his sweet wife and two dear children and treating them as the widow and orphans that they were.

Area churches, let alone the world, were shocked as we cared for this needy family, as we put a roof over their heads and food on their table. They were stunned that we not only refused to send this young girl out into the workplace and her kids into daycare, but that we refused to let Caesar have any part in caring for her. But this is just what the Bible says we are to do. We are witnesses to Him because He is a husband to the widow and a father to the orphan.

Of course our little community has a long way to go. We are far from being odd enough. We still bicker with each other. We still fret and fear over things that do not matter. We still seek the praise of the world. We still live with one foot in this earthly place. The allure of the world is strong.

Our failures, however, are not an excuse for further failure. That we have far to go is no reason not to go; if anything, it is a reason to move more quickly. After all, it was difficult for those in the book of Acts as well. If they could go to the coliseum, not as spectators but as victims—we ought to be able to put up with being thought slightly odd.

We are witnesses. Our sorrows, like His, are not over who wins a basketball game but over husbands who leave their families. And our joys, like His, are not in mere amusement but in reflecting on the glory to which we have been called, in drinking up the glory that is our King. We are to be different, set apart, called out, separate. We are to think more clearly, love more dearly, live more sagely and die more bravely. We are to be like the One Whose name we bear. We are to be faithful in carrying out the continuing acts of Jesus on this earth.

All in favor of family values raise your hands. Have you ever wondered what family values are? Are the fans of family values those who buy the jumbo size detergent at the grocery store? Those who spend the night at motels where kids stay free?

We're all for families, but too often we don't know why. In these pages I have argued that we must begin to put away the worldly wisdom that divides families, that puts each member in its appropriate demographic, and thus grants them an identity. When the world sees my oldest daughter they see an eight-year old girl; that means Barbie, and pretty soon Ricky Martin. But when Darby looks at herself, she sees a Sproul. Her identity is bound up in being a member of our family. To put it another way, she has more in common with this now 35-year-old man than she does with the little girl down the street.

And I have in these pages highlighted all manner of social ills that come from failing to see ourselves as a family, as well as all manner of cultural manners and mores that encourage such destructive thinking. But I hope that I am for families not because the world is for individuals and I'm against what the world is for, but that I am for families because the Bible is for families. I don't want to be reactionary; I want to be biblical.

The Bible demonstrates that it is for families on page one. God did not make a covenant with Adam. Nope, not before the fall, not after the fall. God never made a covenant with Noah, or one with Abraham, Moses, David, not even a covenant with believers. Each and every time a covenant is made between God and man, it is made between God and the man *and* the household *and* as many as are afar off. God makes covenants with families.

But such is not restricted to Hebrew thinking. The same principle applies in the New Covenant, as the covenant goes to the Gentiles. In Acts 16 we have an almost comical example of this. Paul and Silas are in jail, praying and singing. The ground begins to shake; Paul and Silas, and all the prisoners are loosed from their chains. In runs the jailer like sleepy-eyed Barney Fife, ready to put that one bullet in his head. But Paul stops him, telling him that none have escaped.

The jailer calls for a light, runs to Paul and Silas in tears and asks, "Sirs, what must I do to be saved?" This is no Jew. He thinks just like a twentieth century American—it's all about him. Gotta take care of number one. He forgets his family while contemplating a suicide that will make of them a widow and orphans. And he forgets them when he begins to look forward with hope.

"So they said, 'Believe on the Lord Jesus Christ, and you will be saved, you and your household.'" He asked the wrong question, but they gave him the right answer. Now we see the biblical idea of covenants and families making its way into the Gentile community. They must stop thinking like American individualists; they must begin to see their own organic unity with their family, the way God sees it.

We are told next that all of the jailer's house heard the gospel preached, that he and his house were baptized, and they had a feast in celebration of all the household having believed God.

Does that mean that there are two ways into heaven, that either one must believe on the Lord, or that one must be the child of one who believes?

Of course not. It seems rather likely that after a generation of two, if not in that first one, we would have discovered that not all jailer children were jailer children, as not all Israel was Israel. I would expect to find covenant breakers in the family. But that's what they are—covenant breakers. They aren't little halfway covenant children who failed to make it all the way in.

Neither were they all the way in but somehow slipped from God's hands and lost their salvation. Rather, as those bearing the mark of the covenant—baptism—we are to assume that they were in the one covenant, that covenant by which men are redeemed. And if they repudiated the faith that one must hold to be redeemed, to be in the covenant, then they were never really in, and so are covenant breakers.

It's not that complicated. We only have trouble with this because we still think like the jailer first thought. We know we are justified by faith alone; we know that without faith there is no salvation. And yet even in our day we see children getting the mark of salvation who later end up outside the camp. Just as with the Jews.

When a child was circumcised in the Old Testament, no one said a prayer hoping the child would one day be in covenant with God. Nobody spent the next six to twelve years resting in the soft pillow of the strange notion of an age of accountability. Nobody stayed up nights over that same time frame waiting, and hoping and praying that when that child was older he would make a decision. Nobody let out a great sigh of relief when the child stood before the temple and made a profession. He wore his profession everywhere he went; when he repudiated it he was cut off, just like his 8-day-old foreskin.

As did the family of the Philippian jailer, and as we do—at least those of us who bring our children to the water. One covenant, unavoidable, and we either keep it in faith—which we never really know—or we break it. For us and our families, and for as many as are afar off. His grace is boundless, from generation to generation. Paul and Silas sang of it. The jailer rejoiced in it. If only we believed it.

The Democrats now control the Senate. Joseph Biden has been placed at the head of the Senate Foreign Relations Committee. Suppose that Senator Biden schedules time to debate and to pass the United Nations Treaty on Children's Rights. Suppose that the treaty passes and becomes law, as it has in over 150 other nations around the globe. It will then be illegal to spank your child. It will then be illegal to choose against the wishes of the child where your child will go to school. It will then be illegal to enter the child's bedroom without the child's permission. You will be unable to require your child to attend Lord's Day worship with you. What will you do?

These suppositions are not at all a stretch. I think it extremely likely that in the next ten years the UN treaty will be passed by the Senate. And remember that according to the Constitution, international treaties that are duly passed supersede all other laws of the land. What will you do?

The Apostle Paul wrote to the citizens living under the gentle rule of imperial Rome: "Let every soul be subject to the governing authorities. For there is no authority except from God, and the authorities that exist are appointed by God. Therefore whoever resists the authority resists the ordinances of God, and those who resist bring judgment on themselves" (Romans 13:1-2).

I know it's hard to believe, but there it is. And probably a good thing—if God had not made this absolutely clear, no doubt the Sproul home would be the Sproul compound, and would by now have become a part of the lore of the black helicopter crowd.

There is, however, a limit to almost all authority. No authority, whether it be the authority of a husband over a wife, or that of a parent over a child, or that of a session over a family, or that of a presbytery over a session, or that of a government over any of the above, may act directly against the One who gave that authority. The one exception, of course, is God Himself; the only limit on His authority is Himself.

This autonomous God has told us that we are to raise our children in the nurture and admonition of the Lord (Ephesians 6), that we are to continually instruct them in righteousness (Deuteronomy 6), that we are to drive folly far from them through the use of the rod (Proverbs 22). And soon, it appears, this false god, the state deified in the United Nations, will tell us that we may not.

An account in Acts gives us wisdom on the issue. Remember that in chapter 3 Peter has healed a lame man who had been seeking alms outside the temple. This was not done in a corner. Peter then delivers his second sermon, and Peter and John are arrested under duress from the Sanhedrin.

Knowing they can't really hurt them, for too many had witnessed the miracle, the Sanhedrin instead command the two to preach no more in the name of Jesus. The response of Peter and John is familiar to us: "Whether it is right in the sight of God to listen to you more than to God, you decide" (Acts 4:19). They flatly refused to obey the Sanhedrin; God had commanded them to preach, and so they would.

The principle that the church has derived from this event is rather simple on its face—we are to obey all authorities over us unless or until they command us to do that which God forbids, or forbid us to do that which God commands. When they tell us to kill our babies, as the state does in China, we are to refuse. When they forbid us to spank our children, we are to do so anyway.

My concern over the U.N. Treaty on Children's Rights is not that I will be left unable to raise my children as God has commanded, or that I will face the wrath of the state for doing so. My concern is that too many in the evangelical church will roll over and obey the state, will fail to follow the heroic example of Peter and John.

I am not concerned that, if and when this happens, it will be a sign that God has fallen asleep at the switch. Paul's principle in Romans 13:2 still applies—whatever the state requires, even if what they require is in contradiction to the law of God, it requires because God ordained it.

When the Babylonians took Jerusalem, they did so because God ultimately sent them to do so in judgment. The Babylonians didn't know that; they did it because they were evil. But God did know. And the pious Jew would have likewise known that God had sent them, and would still have fought to the death. That God ordains circumstances should not change our call to obey His law, including the law which tells us that we must fight with all our strength against the very circumstances that He has ordained.

For most of the history of these United States, the question of civil disobedience and the Christian has been a hypothetical one. For most of that history God has blessed us with comparative peace and comparatively righteous rule. But such is no longer the case.

We would be wise to consider these things before Nebuchadnezzer builds his statue and commands us to bow. We would be wise to gird up our loins before the battle actually begins. We would be wise to prepare ourselves for the consequences of disobeying man in our obedience to God. We would be wise to remember the faith of those three wise young men who boldly told the king: "O Nebuchadnezzer, we have no need to answer you in this matter. If that is the case, our God whom we serve is able to deliver us from the burning fiery furnace, and He will deliver us from your hand, O king. But if not, let it be known to you, O king, that we do not serve your gods, nor will we worship the gold image which you have set up" (Daniel 3:17-18).

CHAPTER 10

Reverence

❧

And one cried to another and said:
"Holy, holy, holy is the LORD of hosts;
the whole earth is full of His glory!"

❧

Isaiah 6:3

I s nothing sacred anymore? On a rhetorical level the answer seems to be: no, nothing is. But the question itself challenges its own premise, as we ask it so often, in such a flippant way, that we no longer even take desecration seriously.

On a more straightforward level the answer is: of course. It is the very nature of the sacred that it is unbesmirched by the vicissitudes of a given era. The "anymore" part doesn't belong; that which was sacred remains sacred. To be sacred is to be transcendent, and so safely out of reach of the most diligent of graffiti artists. Does anybody treat anything sacredly anymore? Perhaps not. Is anything sacred? Most definitely.

The world creates its own sacred objects, because, as Paul tells us in Romans 1, man is incurably religious. We fashion something with our hands and then bow down before it. When the Senate debates the merits of a Constitutional Amendment to ban desecrating—which means to make unsacred, or to treat as unsacred—the flag, they are acting not as legislators but as priests of the state religion (which worships the state), calling their council to pronounce canon law about that which is sacred. When one is expelled from academic society for suggesting that perhaps that secular saint Martin Luther King was guilty of academic fraud and marital fraud, we know what is considered sacred. When one good old boy yells "Earnhardt!' and receives the reply from another good old boy "Stinks!"—I know, I know, but I'm writing for a family audience—we see two rival witch doctors each trying to put the whammy on the religion of the other. When one announces that there is too an objective truth, and that relativism is a lie, one not only desecrates but defenestrates the most sacred of cultural cows.

The church responds in one of three ways. The most common response is—surprise, surprise—to do the same thing. We have our own sacred cows. Who do you think is driving the movement to make the flag sacred but the Christian right? And while we might speak ill of Dr. King, woe betide the fool who should ever speak a word against Billy Graham. I still hold the record at

World magazine for the article which prompted the most mail. In that article I humbly stood by the gospel and challenged Dr. Graham's assurance to the nation in the wake of the Oklahoma City bombing that all the little children who died there were in heaven. And even in the Reformed camp one must be careful to presuppose the inerrancy of Dr. Van Til.

A second response to the sacred is that we make clear distinctions between the sacred and the secular. This view holds that if there's no Bible verse saying such and such is a good thing, then forget about it. These are the missionaries who ship their little children off to boarding school so that they can do the work of the ministry. These are the Protestant flagellants who eat their parsley potatoes and their Wonder bread, and become suspicious of those who use pepper. These are the good folks our friends at *Credenda/Agenda* like to call "amillennial Gnostics." The sacred, which consists of prayer and Bible reading, is good; everything else is bad. And won't it be great when we get to heaven so we can pray and read our Bibles all day long? And won't it be even better when we don't have these pesky bodies to get in our way and tempt us with pleasure?

The third response is to treat nothing as sacred. The idea of the sacred is anathema to the pagans we are trying to reach. They wallow in the muck; and our response, because we love them so, is to do the same. We play the realism game, doing our best to offend any sensible sensibility, all in order to be with it. This is seen in the dumbing down of our worship, where we try to make Sunday look as much like every other day as possible, only worse. We throw on our cut-offs, blow out our flip-flops, step on a pop-top, and saunter down to the local meeting place to hear some hip comic tell us that God is just a regular guy like us, only better.

Of course not one of these approaches is biblical. Whether we treat the unsacred as sacred, or the sacred as unsacred, we fail to judge rightly. In some sense everything not sin is sacred. When I sit down to eat a cheeseburger and fries I am enjoying the bounty of our God; that's why I pause to give Him thanks. And when I am splitting wood for the fire I am also performing two sacred tasks—the task of exercising dominion over creation, and the task of providing for the family God has entrusted to me. And it is a good thing to remember that such is true. Our lives only seem mundane to us when we fail to see them in their true context, the context of glorifying God and enjoying Him forever.

But at the same time we must remember that some things are more sacred than others. When I kneel at the Lord's Table I am again enjoying the bounty of our God. And I must again give thanks. But I am enjoying so much more than the provision of daily bread. I do not live on bread alone; I also feed upon the body of Christ, and enjoy a closer fellowship with Him than I do at McDonald's. When I teach my children to obey, I engage in a sacred task; but such is not as sacred as when I place upon them the mark of Christ at baptism. These are sacraments because they are sacred. And they are sacred because they are holy. And because they are holy, they are set apart, and we are to revere them.

It is our ignorance of and hatred toward the Old Testament that causes this problem. We know that in the New Testament the Pharisees made a big fuss about what was clean or unclean. And we know that the Pharisees were the bad guys. Therefore, we wisely conclude that all these distinctions are wicked—thereby making the distinction that the making of distinctions is unclean—forgetting that as with all the law of God, the trouble with the Pharisees was not that they obeyed God's law, but that they disobeyed it and made up their own. I'm not arguing for keeping kosher; I am saying that the making of distinctions is a biblical idea. Egalitarianism, on the other hand, smells like sulfur—which is to say, like rotten eggs.

That all things are sacred—and that some are more sacred than others—means, of course, that we have a sacred duty to assess accurately the sacredness of various things. To treat a thing as more sacred or less sacred than it actually is, is to love something more or less than we ought to love it.

C.S. Lewis argues that all sin is a failure to love *ordinately*—that means *in order*. When I love my dog more than I love my wife (which, of course, I would never do, because my dog is a money pit; when she isn't eating my chickens she is getting herself hurt enough to require an expensive trip to the vet) I cannot excuse myself by pointing out what a great and glorious thing love is. In affirming that wine is a great gift of God I do not give myself a license to swim in it. Love does not forgive everything.

But we also get into trouble when we don't love or revere things enough. When I gossip about my friends I am failing to revere them, to think them more important than myself. When I tell little lies, puffing up my accomplishments, I show a severe lack of reverence for the truth.

I do the same, by the way, when I determine never to study anything controversial or to talk of such matters because they can break the peace; I'm revering peace more than I should, truth less than I should. When I sit down for a night of Must See TV, I not only spend the evening laughing at the desecration of any number of things God calls holy—families, marriage, sex—but I also show a severe lack of reverence for time; what's three hours in the grand scheme of things?

Isn't it ironic that we defend our desecration of the little things with the argument that they are part of a bigger thing? Because the big thing—say, eternity—is so big, we reason that the little thing—say, three hours—is so little. We ought to revere time precisely because it is a part of eternity, just as we are to revere each other, little tiny people that we are, because we bear God's image, and He is not so tiny.

We are a people stuck in neutral. We have made everything so commonplace, having been there and done that, that our problem is not so much a passion for evil but an evil lack of passion for anything at all. Far better to live in a world in which the answer to the question, "Is nothing sacred?" is, "Of course, the holy, esteemed dog's backside is sacred, and death will fall swiftly on any who speak ill of the exalted backside of the dog." Such would be a people, like the foolish Greeks at Mars Hill, who at least have the sense to worship something, who at least see that something is more important than their personal peace and affluence. And the solution to their problem is not to persuade them that nothing is really all that important, but to shift their adoring gaze from the creature to the Creator. Instead, we live in an age in which Jesus is just all right with me.

We ought to be trying to show the holiness. When we seek to live simply we are trying to see the mystery, and therefore the holiness of life, which is horribly shrouded by the deadly efficiency of the seamless process from Archer-Daniels-Midland to the processing plant to the cannery to the distributor to the store shelves, through the scanner and into our microwaves. When we seek to live separately we are trying to live holy lives, which is what holiness is all about. We want to be set apart, distinguished, and so go through our lives not swimming in the lukewarm poison of quiet desperation, but rather swimming upstream with all the determination of a salmon whose biological clock is ticking. When we try to live deliberately we are trying to order our loves, to determine what things to value and how much to value them, through the wisdom of the prophets rather than through the madmen of Madison Avenue in search of their profits.

We at the Center don't need to add drama to our lives by living vicariously through the denizens of the world of the soaps; the drama is already there if we will but see it. We are not replacing light bulbs and changing diapers in monotonous drudgery; we are fighting the great war, beating back sin from our garden as if it were a voracious, creeping weed. We don't need to manufacture holy moments, for they are all around us. We don't need to bungee jump or skydive in order to give our lives the thrill that they are missing; we need only to realize that we are at work building the holy Kingdom of our holy King.

Every day is jihad—holy war. And as such every day is both war and holy, and all the moments therein. And when we forget that truth, when we kick back and relax, we are losing the battle, a battle that has already been won.

Perhaps no slogan better captures the folly of our age than this one: "Been there, done that." There are postures or moods that tend to dominate given cultures at given times. When you think of the Victorian age you think, rightly or wrongly, of stuffed shirts, stiff upper lips and haughty manners. When you think of the sixties what comes to mind is a bedraggled, patchwork doll with a hazy and placid grin. We live now in the age of a sneer too slack to frighten.

The post-modern age, however, is an age of cynicism, the younger and far more sinister brother of modernism's skepticism. It is one thing to doubt the truth claim of another, to withhold judgment until all necessary tests and cross-checks have been performed; it is another thing altogether to merely sneer and scoff at the truth claim merely because it is a truth claim.

The anti-epistemology that is at the heart of postmodernism is at once sophisticated and ludicrously idiotic. There are well paid men and women sitting in endowed chairs of philosophy who write learned articles about relativism, this idea that there is no objective truth. They throw around impressive-sounding words and phrases like phenomenology, meta-cognition, and textual narrative contexts, all in a vain attempt to hide the fact that they are really just saying, "It is an absolute truth that there is no absolute truth." They are desperately at work trying to hide the fact that they have cut out their eyes to spite their sight. And they bid us to see this as wisdom.

Such nonsense makes its way into our everyday lives in a host of ways. We embrace it when convenient, when we are tired of arguing—"Well, the snow may be wet to you, but it's not to me, so there." We defend it when we are tired of defending ourselves or our friends from moral attacks—"Who is to say that it is wrong to engage in sex with a 21-year-old with stars in her eyes who works for you, but is not your wife—and to lie to a grand jury about it? I mean, who is to say?"

But it reaches us in more existential ways as well. Relativism not only decimates truth and banishes morality, but it renders useless *teleology*—our understanding of purpose. That is, we cannot know what is true or what is right, nor can we know what we or anything else is for. We become adrift, with no direction. In short, in a relativistic world, nothing matters, nothing is worth getting worked up over, because nothing is ultimately worth anything at all. That makes us cynics, sitting about in our jaded, plastic garden without a care in the world, and with nothing to care about. We live not in peace but in a catatonic state.

And such is our mood. We are too filled with ennui to even be disturbed by our ennui. Any report of anything exciting, anything moving, anything even worth reporting is met with the moment's mantra—"Been there, done that"—or, more cynical still—"Been there, done that, got the T-shirt."

We cannot, in this age, express any sort of passion. The truly hip would rather be caught with a Spice Girls record than be caught up in some sort of emotion. Emotions are just mental constructs, ones that we know can be manipulated through our constant absorption in entertainment media; in fact, that is the only way to trigger them, through manipulation. To feel emotion, at least without a sense of irony and detachment, is to deny that nothing matters. And to deny that, you are faced with the Arbiter of what matters—a value-giving (and law-giving) God. And He might just want something from us—like obeisance.

To be earnest in any way is to expose oneself not merely to an argument against that which one is earnest about, but to raw ridicule for the crime of being earnest. It's all been done before, and nothing really came out of it anyway, so why make a fuss? The latest news then is that there is no news. But not to worry; it doesn't matter anyway.

This is the cynicism to which the Preacher fell in his journey through Ecclesiastes. There is nothing new under the sun. And everything old under the sun is going the way of all flesh. And this is where our culture's long journey under the sun has brought it. Our culture has reached the end of its rope, and is too bored to even tie a noose and put an end to it all. And so it will go out not with a bang, but with a whimper.

Christians, however, are not citizens of this world; our address lies over the rainbow and beyond the sun. Our response needs to be *contra mundum*—against the world. We need a deadly earnestness that is antithetical to the deadly apathy of the world. We need to be a people who care, who care deeply.

And that means jettisoning our own cynicism. The irony is this—our ironic age had taught us the cynicism we need, in order to be cynical about cynicism. But we must not stay there, spending all our time being against being indifferent, but rather we must spend our time being *for* the Kingdom of God. We must rejoice without self-consciousness over the birth of a new covenant child. We must weep with a sincerity that hurts. We must love with vigor, and hate with equal passion. We must accept the slings and arrows of those who would call us simple and innocent.

In the biblical culture, things *do* matter. Battles are fought and soldiers are wounded. And all the battles end with the triumph of the King. And then we face our ineffable future of beholding His ineffable glory for eternity. If we can't be earnest about that, we have been born only once, and born dead.

You see them all around you, but you don't know what they are. They could be office buildings for mid-sized companies; they could be shopping malls. The only giveaway is the sign; though there is rarely an oak or a river in sight, the sign says "River Oaks Worship Center." Step inside and you won't see worship either.

You know the kind of buildings I'm talking about. They are essentially as windowless as they are shapeless. If you're in the nice part of town the outside is covered in faux brick. If it's not such a great part of town all you see is the sheet metal on the outside. Inside you'll find the magic—one large room that can comfortably seat hundreds of spectators and can be configured for a basketball game, a daycare center or a laser show, along with a sound system that costs more than the building.

We are, after all, Americans. The only indigenous philosophy we have come up with so far is pragmatism, the unworkable idea that we are to judge all ideas by whether they work or not. No one wants to put the church into debt for a building used only one day a week; no, it is far better to go into debt for a building used several days a week. And the fastest way out of debt is to disguise the fact that it's a church, so we can attract more yuppies who give—but only if we have the programs and the entertainment they crave. We're too enlightened and modern to believe that there could be such a thing as sacred space. We don't go in for architectural iconophilia. So we smash the icons. We pave paradise and put up a parking lot.

Buildings are not magic. We remember God's warning to the children of Israel—that no building, no matter how grand, can contain Him. But they do *matter*, because they are a medium with a message. Buildings that say 'stodgy' speak of a stodgy god, just as buildings that are hip speak of a hip god. And buildings that look like businesses often become businesses. And those who go there tend to think like customers, viewing not only the church but God Himself as a provider of goods and services. Pragmatic church buildings exist to serve pragmatic gods.

So what do we at the Highlands Study center do? Saint Peter Presbyterian Church, where most of our community gathers to worship, once met in a building that had been a dentist's office. And it looked like a dentist's office. We would have loved having a cathedral, and the people to fill it, but such is what we could afford at the time.

But we did not worship a dental god. Buildings do matter, but they do not determine where we worship. No matter how bad the building might be, if we remember where we really are, we will worship instead of shop. For we actually worship in a place more magnificent than a thousand Notre Dames and more eternal than Saint Peter in the eternal city of Rome.

All Christians, whether we know it or not, gather every Lord's Day at His house, at the heavenly and eternal temple. And such should drive us to our knees; it certainly rules out comedy hour. Consider the seraphim in Isaiah 6. These are the creatures that live in that holy temple, whose job it is to sing the eternal anthem: "Holy, holy, holy is the Lord of hosts: the whole earth is full of His glory." These are creatures who have never known sin from the time of their creation; they have not violated the law of God a single time. When they gather they do indeed love God with all their being. Yet Isaiah tells us that these same seraphim cover both their eyes and their feet with their wings, as they serve in the immediate presence of God. There is no ease here, no casual camaraderie; instead there is a deep consciousness of the infinitely deep chasm that separates creature from Creator.

How much more must we enter into His presence with fear? In ourselves we are nothing but sin. Of course we are covered in the righteousness of Christ; but the angels don't need even that covering—and still they fear. I fear that we do not worship in reverence because we don't know where we are. God is here. And we are but creatures.

Recently I was asked why we at Saint Peter Presbyterian Church kneel when we come to the Lord's Table during our worship; some feared that such was Popish and superstitious. I explained that Presbyterians are not Zwinglians—we do not think that the Lord's Supper is a mere memorial. Neither are we Roman or Lutheran, affirming that Christ's body and blood are actually present with us. In fact, even if such were the case we would not bow to His body and blood because they are properties of His humanity, and thus cannot be worshipped.

Instead we affirm the real presence of the Lord at the table, again not because He descends to Bristol every Lord's Day, but because He lifts us up to Him. We're not bowing because His body is in the elements; we're bowing because our bodies are in His presence, in a more real and special way than in our ordinary lives. I suggested that, if we could, the correct posture at such a meeting would not to be kneeling, but to be dug in beneath the floorboards, quaking.

As I have said before, such doesn't mean that our worship lacks joy; in fact, we can only know joy in our worship when we know who we are and Whom we are with. Happiness, pleasantness, you can have that in any room—but joy is found only in the presence of God. In like manner, you can learn all manner of things about God in a classroom. You can enjoy His people at a picnic. But when we gather to worship we are not seeking to meet the seekers where they are, but to meet the Finder where He is. When we gather on His day we gather to worship, and to worship only.

CHAPTER II

Assumptions

&

*The wisdom of the prudent
is to understand his way;
but the folly of fools is deceit.*

cs

Proverbs 14:8

The unexamined life, Socrates told us, is not worth living. The trouble, of course, is that one cannot reach such a conclusion without first examining one's life. Those out there living worthless lives have at their advantage that they don't know their lives are worthless; they go merrily about their worthless business, ignorant that they are wasting their time and ours. Examining our lives, according to Socrates, is a necessary condition for a worth-*ful* life. If our lives are not worthless we know at least this much about them—that we examine them.

I agree with Socrates, but would add to his thought these thoughts. First, when we are examining our lives we need to avoid looking only inward. Our lives do not consist merely in our own solipsistic thought world. They include the created order, our friends, families and neighbors. And I would add also that there is a ratio involved here. One cannot ask oneself "Do I examine my life?"—answer back, "Yes, I must because I just asked myself that question."—and then go back to watching "So You Want to Be a Millionaire," content that one's life is indeed meaningful. The more we examine our lives, the more meaning there is.

Most of us live in the in-between. We want to have meaningful lives, but we're also rather conscious of that competing aphorism: "Ignorance is bliss." We recognize the importance of examining our lives, but know enough of ourselves that we don't want to look too closely, because we often don't like what we find. When we look deep into that heart of darkness we find— darkness. And when we look deep into the starry sky we see there the radiance of the holiness of God. And that's a contrast that we can do without.

With the conviction of our sin comes the knowledge of the command to repentance. And that means change, something we tend to find off-putting, and so put off. Add to that our knowledge that we stand before God in the righteousness of Christ, and we remain fat and happy. It has been said rightly of the biblical gospel that if our understanding of it doesn't sound like antinomianism, we're not saying it right. The proper anti-dote to antinomianism is not to create a gospel of works but to affirm the biblical truth that we are saved unto good works. We haven't been redeemed so that we can go to heaven; we have been declared righteous so that we can become righteous.

The incessant biblical commands to pursue righteousness—and here, by the way, most of our attention is directed inward, trying to get the mote out of our own eyes—are there not as a means of salvation but as the fruit of salvation; but such makes them no less than commands. Christians still have to do it, even if such is not the ground of our salvation.

We are fulfilling the law of Christ, as Paul writes to those chronic legalists the Galatians: "Brethren, if a man is overtaken in any trespass, you who are spiritual restore such a one in a spirit of gentleness, considering yourself, lest you also be tempted. Bear one another's burdens, and so fulfill the law of Christ. For if anyone thinks himself to be something, when he is nothing, he deceives himself. But let each one examine his own work, and then he will have rejoicing in himself alone, and not in another. For each shall bear his own load" (Galatians 4:1-5).

The legalism of the Galatians was two-fold: first, they added to God's law what He does not require; second, that addition was deemed to be a part of the ground of our salvation. That's the silly part, as if God would stand in judgment over us and announce, "Well, I see all your sins were dealt with at Calvary, and I see that you, by virtue of your union with My Son, have fully obeyed all My law, so welc—wait! What's this? You still have a foreskin? Straight to hell with you, you old goat!" But what Paul did not find fault with was that they encouraged one another to obedience; only we find fault.

And, ironically, we Christians find fault with others because we don't examine our own lives. That is, we yell at people who yell at us, not because of our commitment to the Bible, but because we live in a relativistic culture. Sure, we paint it as "loving one another" or "judge not," but the truth is that we're uncomfortable encouraging one another to righteousness because we ourselves are worldly. Because we do not search our own hearts and root out all the lies of the world that we find there, the one killer weed takes deep root—the one saying that he who points out the weeds in *your* heart is a heartless Pharisee, one who is to be roundly condemned rather than heard out.

Nevertheless, that's what I'm here to tell you. It is with a gentle spirit that I mock the spirit of this world, even when and where it lives in you and me. I don't mind being considered a Pharisee, being called harsh and judgmental. I don't mind not because I am a Pharisee, but because that's what it takes to get the weeds out. As I enjoin you to live a more deliberate life, I am encouraging you to look deep within yourself, to seek out those weeds of the world that lurk there in the dark corners, those unspoken and too often unexamined assumptions that have no biblical foundation. The world's ideas find good soil in our wicked hearts.

I know that the weeds grow well there because of my own self-evaluation. Another lie from the world that has flourished in the church is this one—it is sheer hypocrisy to judge any sins of which the judger is himself guilty. Because we believe that lie, when I come and sound the alarm of worldliness, too many of my readers think I'm saying I have this thing licked, that my garden is pristine.

Quite the opposite is true—I'm concerned about the depth and power of worldliness in the church because I am so well acquainted with the depth and power of worldliness in my own heart. I preach against my own sins because I know them so well. If you want someone to preach against grumbling against God in the midst of severe persecution, go find yourself a Christian in the Sudan. And I'd suggest that you also have him preach to the persecuted Sudanese, not us fat and happy Americans. The American church is afflicted not with suffering but with prosperity; we are not guilty of morbid introspection, but moribund introspection.

As my friend Laurence is wont to say, we are born into a particular time. And, as the Bible says, we are born sinners. And so as we enter this world we come not just with ten fingers and toes, but with a meadow full of dandelions in our hearts. Every day as we move about this pagan world those ideas are watered and nurtured. The dandelions turn to seed and are carried forth to multiply. As we sit in front of the glowing one-eyed brain-eraser we are giving Miracle-Grow to our hidden assumptions. As we surround ourselves with more noises, more distractions, more busyness, we are only averting our senses lest we see that our garden is not edenic but satanic.

It is only a shallow evaluation, however, that recognizes the dandelions and seeks to solve the problem with a lawn mower. When we merely lop the heads off the little monsters we find that they only multiply. We know we're not supposed to say that we live for the latest toy, but we don't tear the problem up by the root. We know we're not supposed to say that we just want to be entertained, but we'll never listen to a boring sermon on the subject. No, we need to get at the root, and it takes a sharp plow to break up cold, hard earth. We need to dig up the whole thing carefully, lest we leave some of the weed behind to grow again.

They are out there—or rather, in here—those subterranean monsters that lurk beneath the surface but are busy shaping the very ground that we walk on. Everywhere we go we carry with us the seeds of our own destruction. And we need to get rid of them. We need to have the zeal of the professional soldier, not the haphazard indifference of the weekend warrior. We need almost to be frantic, to not rest until they are driven away. We need to not be satisfied with our puny and occasional victories; we need to take every thought captive. That's not some thought, or even most thoughts, but every thought. The labor is hard, and the labor is painful—but the labor is fruitful.

And let us not forget that our Father, the great Gardener who delights in pruning us that He might make us more fruitful, has not set us to do this work empty-handed. He has given us tools—powerful tools—to use in that work. He has given us His Word that serves to expose the weeds, that works as a mirror showing us where we fall short. He has given us the sacraments that remind us that the job will one day be finished and we will eat with the King. He has given us one another, commanding us to spur one another on to good works. And most important, he has given us His Spirit, who delights to work holiness in us, who is growing us into men and women who love God with all our heart, mind, soul and strength. We cannot afford to leave these tools rusting on the wall. They, unlike any other tools, become stronger and more effective with greater use.

As we pull up the weeds in our garden, we find that we too flourish. We find that we are growing in grace, for it is He who is working in us both to do and to will His good pleasure. The weeds lose their power to choke out the fruit we are called to produce. We don't want empty gardens, but gardens flowering with fruit.

That's the connection with the purpose statement of the Highlands Study Center, which is: to help Christians live more simple, separate and deliberate lives to the glory of God and for the building of His kingdom. All that we do is kingdom building. All that we do is the exercise of dominion, the tending of the garden.

So if I poke you in the eye with either sword or trowel, please don't take offense. All it means is that one of us has a weed to pull. If I tromped on a flower, thinking it a weed, then my thinking needs to be corrected. (By the way, I love mail. I believe in encouraging each other unto good works enough that I love to be corrected). But if I tromp on a weed that you thought a flower—for goodness sake, be happy about it.

We need each other; and that rugged individualism whereby we go it alone, confident in our ability to examine our lives sufficiently without loving friends—that too is one of the weeds that comes from the world, not a flower that comes from the Word. We ought to take offense when our friends are silent, not when they tell us about the dandelions. They didn't put them there, and pretending they aren't there doesn't make them go away.

Get your hands dirty. Look at yourself and see if these things are not true. Remember as we consider the truth that we are slaves to our subterranean presuppositions, that it is the truth that sets us free.

The world is awash in competing images of the family. When I say "Father Knows Best", most of us immediately conjure up the image of middle class stability, of a man with his nose buried in the newspaper and a woman in pearls serving up cookies. When I say "The Simpsons", those impious enough to watch it but pious enough to admit it know immediately what kind of family I am talking about, a hapless father with his nose buried in the television and a blue haired lady serving up beer to him.

Both images, however, are somewhat dated. The modern image of the family is of a group of friends. They care for each other but their ties do not bind. They sip fancy coffee, crack wise at each other and serve only their own needs.

But most of us know at least to be somewhat on our guard when the blue-eyed monster is let loose in our homes. We know that Hollywood is trying to sell us something, and, based on their product line, we prefer to choose the laughs and skip the world view. Of course, it seeps in a little bit. Don't think I don't know that when I use sarcasm against the folly of postmodernism that I am feeding the hand that bites me. A little worldliness is a small price to pay for so many laughs.

One reason we know these celluloid family images aren't telling the truth is that they don't match our experience. None of our fathers wore a tie and a cardigan sweater after work. None of our brothers called our fathers "Homer." And everyone knows that large, two-bedroom apartments in New York City cost significantly more than one can make drinking coffee all day.

The greater danger is that we allow our own experience to shape our understanding of the family. Our unspoken assumptions often come not from the television but from the hearth of our youth. My father tells a story of the tensions this can cause in a marriage. Both my grandfathers were businessmen who traveled from time to time. Soon after my parents were married it came time for my father's first business trip. He politely asked my saintly mother to pack his suitcase—at which point she went into a slow boil. My father, of course, was baffled—not only because baffled is what men always become in the face of an angry woman, but also because of his expectation that she pack his suitcase.

The problem isn't limited to dividing up household chores—though that's a big deal. Denise's father is amazingly helpful around the house. Compared to my father I'm Mr. Mom; compared to her father I'm Archie Bunker. So while I'm looking for Denise to take out a full page ad in USA Today to brag on what a sweetheart I am, she's wondering when I'm going to get busy.

These unspoken and too often unexamined assumptions can touch every aspect of the home. Some women measure their femininity just as their mothers did, by accumulating as many cute knick-knacks for the home as can be crammed into a curio cabinet; others measure it by how many pennies can be squeezed out of the coupon section of the local paper. Some men measure their masculinity by how many hours a week they can put in at the office, others by how loud they can belch.

These assumptions not only cause conflict among members of the family, they can also cause internal conflict. The truth is that even if we examine the assumptions, even if we recognize that some of them don't belong, it doesn't make them magically disappear. I know the Bible doesn't teach that the measure of a man is found by the size of his ministry. I know that what makes my father a great man is stuff his many fans know nothing about, and—sadly—care less about. But as I aspire to be a godly man like my father, still lurking in the back of my mind is this notion that to be a man you must be godly—and be admired and read by boodles of Reformed people.

So here's my solution. When I find myself down because I've failed to exorcise all the patently false unspoken assumptions in my head about what it means to be a man—I just let myself be sad. It's a kind of penance. "If you're fool enough to care about that nonsense," I tell myself, "then you deserve the sadness."

But the better solution is to bury ourselves in the Word of God. The more we listen to God tell us what a family is, the more we will put to death the lies of the devil. It's not magic, it's not instant—that's also a lie from the culture. But it is daily work.

The right image is not on old TV, new TV, nor even most probably in the home of your youth. The answer is found in the Bible. We need to measure ourselves not against Robert Young, Homer Simpson, or even our own fathers, but we need to measure ourselves by our elder Brother.

And as we get frustrated by the lingering lies, we need to remember that He is at work in us, that He is sowing the seed of the fruit of His Spirit. We need to remember that one day this will all end and we will not only want to be as He is, but we *will* be as He is, for we shall see Him as He is. Our true and eternal Father has so promised.

Patriotism is a learned behavior, sort of. It is learned in the sense that it is not something innate. It's not as though we are born with a deep love of sin and a deep love of our country.

But it's not a learned behavior in the sense that such is something we study; rather it is something that comes to us through a host of unconscious mechanisms. It comes on us, but in the same way that the flu virus comes upon us. Only it is more debilitating.

Among the issues in the school wars is the issue of history. On the left are a host of historical revisionists who use the discipline as a means to insert their liberal assumptions into the heads of the little tykes. There is a more passive version of this and a more aggressive. The more passive is the mere ignoring of our history; here students are taught more than anyone could possibly want to know about George Washington Carver, all the while learning nothing at all about George Washington. The more aggressive will tell us about George Washington, but it's all bad news; the kids are warned not to be like George, because of all his right-wing views.

'Conservatives' object to this new kind of propaganda. They insist instead on the same old propaganda that they got when they were in school. They want the tykes to learn about what a bunch of saints our founding fathers were. These parents want their children to genuflect any time the name of an approved hero is mentioned. The left wants a daily litany of repentance for all politically incorrect crimes; the right wants all the children to proclaim their faith in the state.

My concern, as usual, is not so much with the loony left; I'd rather have children learn to be suspicious of the state for all the wrong reasons than learn to love their country for all the wrong reasons. Rather, my concern is with the truth that we respond to the important matter of how we view our country without thinking. We feel, and feel strongly, but we do not do so deliberately. And when the right plays into this, it creates slaves rather than lovers of freedom. When we adopt the tools of the left, we find ourselves sliding their way in a hurry.

I noticed this phenomenon years ago when I held the conviction that one ought not to vote. I reached that conviction (which I have since jettisoned) because of my belief in the power of the vote. I didn't vote because I took the power of the vote more seriously than those who did vote. I couldn't make myself vote for Republicans because I would feel responsible for the things that they did. The Social Security tax increase that Reagan passed—that would be my fault. And the Americans with Disabilities

Act—it would end up on me if I voted for George Bush. Those Supreme Court justices appointed by those men who refuse to protect the unborn would have been placed there by me. I take seriously those bumper stickers that read, "Don't Blame Us, We Voted For Jeff Davis."

But what struck me as I sought to persuade others of this point of view was the almost robotic response: "You…must…vote.…You…have…a…duty…to…vote." It often came out like some magic mantra. And when I asked why I had to vote, I got a repeat of the mantra. "It…is…your…duty." It was rather scary. There was no evidence brought forth as to where this duty came from, no verses quoted to demonstrate that God requires this. There was only the repetition of the thesis.

My theory was that these folks had been brainwashed. And I still believe it. The same thing continues to happen when I challenge the notion of pledging allegiance to the flag. What struck me there first was the assumption by my friends that I had the burden in this argument. Somehow people opposite me in this debate seemed to think that it was my duty prove that we shouldn't do it—which I was happy to do—rather than their duty to defend this solemn vow they wanted me to take. It seems natural to us to swear allegiance to a flag, and the non-existent republic for which it stands, but only because we've all done it so many times. It seems normal because they made us do it every day when we were too little to argue about it.

Suppose that every child in the country every day of the week patted their head and rubbed their tummy. Don't you think that we'd still all do it as adults? Wouldn't people look at you funny if you suggested that such wasn't necessary? Don't you think such would be frightening? Suppose that all our land was taxed to pay for having this done. I'm not suggesting that horrible things would happen if we all rubbed our tummies and patted our heads. Maybe some good would come out of it—fewer full-headed men to make me envious. But when we are brainwashed we ought not to be so concerned with the content.

This is how governments operate. We are in the throes of an Orwellian nightmare but dreaming through a Huxleyan dose of *soma*. It is much more efficient to gild a cage than it is to reinforce its doors. And so much harder to persuade the birds to flee their captivity when the birds are trained to sing on cue, like Pavlov's dogs, that they are in the land of the free and the home of the brave.

If you want to be free you must be deliberate. You must search out the unspoken—and too often unexamined—assumptions that frame the course of your thinking on these issues with appropriate fear and loathing over a state that would wash the brains of its littlest citizens. And if you don't want to be free— simply do nothing and think nothing. If the government wants your opinion, they'll give it to you.

Chapter 12

Jihad

❧

For the weapons of our warfare
are not carnal but mighty in God
for pulling down strongholds.

❧

II Corinthians 10:4

War, they tell us, is hell. And they are right in one sense, though wrong in another. Though I have never been in combat, I know that whatever horror is there, though it may be unlike any other earthly horror, it is not hell. Every soldier ever caught in the barrage on Omaha Beach, every survivor of the Bataan Death March, every casualty of Pickett's charge—if they were not covered in the blood of Christ when they died, they would sorely love to be back in the midst of that carnage if it meant an escape from what they are going through now.

But war is hell in another way. The true war, the real war of which all other wars are but a shadow, is the war between heaven and hell.

As with all wars, this war began with a revolt against lawful authority. Satan was displeased with his standing and led a band of angels in a revolution. He, along with a third of all the company of heaven, was banished. Soon after the serpent took up residence in the garden and went looking for recruits. There he succeeded—at least for a time. He added to his battalions the whole of the human race.

God, however, is not a recruiter. His army is staffed strictly with draftees. In His declaration of war He made that promise, that He would draft His soldiers; only One was a volunteer. God spoke to the serpent, "I will put enmity between you and the woman, and between your seed and her Seed: He shall bruise your head and you shall bruise His heel" (Genesis 3:15). This is God's solemn declaration of war, and it is the context of all of our lives.

The devil understands this. Central to his strategy is to make us forget that we are at war, or to confuse the nature of the warfare and the division of the combatants. His weapons too are not merely carnal. He is, after all, more crafty than any of the other beasts.

As I write, the United States government is engaged in a righteous—albeit undeclared—war. It is as far as I can tell rightly wielding the sword to bring to justice those who have waged war against these United States. I'm pleased at the early reports that American soldiers have thus far been kept safe, that Afghan civilians have been spared by and large, and that great damage is being done to the assets of the Taliban regime. Such is exactly as it should be. I rejoice to see the execution of justice. Over there, things are going well; over here, however, I have some concerns.

First, the devil has fashioned a great victory in confusing us. Most professing believers have fallen even more deeply into that grave syncretistic heresy of confusing the kingdom of God with these United States. The kingdom is indeed here, but no more than it is everywhere else, including Afghanistan.

We have politicians seeming to call out to God for deliverance while Christians call out to the state for deliverance. There is a blurring of who "we" are. Are we the children of God, citizens of heaven, or are we Americans? These are not the same thing. Are we offended because bin Laden assaulted Christians, or because he assaulted consumerist American culture? For which offense are we seeking vengeance?

Second, our syncretism has sunk to new depths. My prayer is that never again will some fool say, "All religions are basically the same." My fear is that in trying to separate Islam from terrorism, so as to allow for continuing religious pluralism, we will affirm with the so-called minister of the gospel who prayed in the National Cathedral to "the God of Moses, Jesus and Moham-med" that all religions that behave nicely are the same.

In like manner I fear that what will be condemned is not Islam but any religion that makes a claim of exclusive truth. After they finish off the Islamic fundamentalists, which funda-mentalists do you think they will come for next?

We are witnessing two armies that share a common denial of the Lordship of Christ making war with one another. Islamic fundamentalism is warring with American relativism—and we, the soldiers of the King, are spectators. Of course we must be compassionate spectators, offering the comfort of Christ to our suffering neighbors. Of course we must be 'active' spectators if in our service to the King we serve also as a soldier of the state. Of course we must honor and encourage the courage of those who are fighting this war, whether they be firemen in New York or bomber pilots over Kabul. Of course we should pray for the peace of this Babylon in which we make our pilgrimage.

But we Christians must remember where we have our citizenship. We must not let ourselves get distracted from the true war. Like Islam we are a people bent on world conquest. We, like they, will not rest until our God is affirmed by all men everywhere. We will not break into that final celebration until every knee bows, and every tongue confesses that Jesus Christ is Lord. We, like they, want to see our Holy book honored and revered—not just here, not just in the west, but in northern Africa, in the Arabian peninsula, in western China and in the near east. We, like they, celebrate our martyrs, those who died fighting faithfully in this war, whether it was in the Sudan, in Iran, or in East Timor. In short, we must not confuse the war of President Bush with our own war.

We Christians need not distinguish between the nice Muslims and the deadly ones, for we understand that both are Christ's enemies. We want to see them both destroyed. And we know it will come to pass. The battle between Allah and Yahweh is the same battle that precedes the garden, for Allah is not just a different name for God, but a different name for the devil. We and they do not worship the same God; for we affirm, to the death, that there is indeed one God—but that Mohammed is not His prophet.

At the same time, however, we Christians are at war with Israel. These are not our cousins, whether they be the socialist and atheistic variety, or the so-called orthodox variety. All who have rejected the Son, no matter how much they protest their love of the Father, are in fact servants of the serpent. Their father is the father of lies.

And so we Christians are likewise at war with the unbelieving

American culture. Whether it be the overt syncretists such as the wolves who presided over the services at the National Cathedral, or the tamer variety, those believers in a civil religion who know nothing about even their own lame god except that he's a big fan of the USA—they are not us. They too are Christ's enemies and must be defeated.

The devil likewise rejoices when we get confused over our weapons. President Bush's war cannot be our war, because he rightly wields a sword. His weapons are carnal, for that is his calling. Our calling, however, is to use the tools that God has given us. We fight the real war, the one in which not mere bodies are at stake but bodies and souls, by proclaiming the gospel.

The gospel we proclaim is the gospel of the kingdom, that Christ rules over all things. The devil, even when he does not silence us, confuses this still more. We cannot win the lost with the gospel when that gospel denies God's sovereignty. If we proclaim a god who wrings his hands over the events of September 11, we have defected. If we proclaim a god who is devoid of wrath and judgment, we make those who believe twice the children of hell that we are. Instead of drafting new soldiers, we merely strengthen the enemy.

The gospel we proclaim, if we want to fight as faithful soldiers, must be a faithful gospel. It must affirm the awful wrath of God that rests upon us, and the promise that if we believe, that same wrath rested upon our King. The gospel we proclaim must affirm that all other gospels are invitations to the wrath of God, gateways to hell.

The gospel we proclaim must also affirm that all those who proclaim the same gospel are our brothers, our fellow soldiers, whether they were once Muslims, Jews, or American yuppies. We are not united under the stars and stripes, but under the scars and stripes. We are one, and no war will divide us. The true war unites us. And so we are one body, the body of Christ the conqueror, who has already overcome the world.

We live in confusing and dangerous times. But greater than

the danger of falling planes or anthrax is the danger of the wrath of God. And so in these times, as in all times, we must think and speak clearly the gospel of the kingdom. When the sky seems to be falling, when everyone seems to have lost their head, when a nation is plunged into uncertainty and doubt—then is the time for faithful proclamation.

When our focus is on the one true war, the confusion crumbles all around us. We are a simple people with a simple message: we all must repent and believe the gospel. We are people of the Book, our simple answer to all great questions. We are people of the simple faith that affirms in all circumstances that we rest in the very hand of God. We do not wring our hands and cry, "How could this happen?" Instead we affirm, just as we do in times of peace and plenty, "It is of the Lord." We are a simple people who will neither spin the truth, nor spin God Himself, because our simple calling is to tell the truth, simply.

When our focus is on the one true war, we are not sucked into the great war frenzy of the nation around us. We adopt neither the confusion of those around us, nor their confused certainty. We neither continue in the folly of relativism—"Who are we to judge the terrorists?"—nor in the folly of jingoism—"Kill them all and let God sort them out."

We are a separate people. What separates us is our convictions, and our lives, that in the very living of them become yet another proclamation of the gospel that has redeemed us. What separates us is not that we are aloof and uncaring, but that we care from a position of peace, and we give of ourselves from that infinite source which is our King.

We honor those in authority over us. We give thanks to God for the blessings of comparative liberty that we enjoy. We revere our forefathers who first won and then defended that liberty. But we are not citizens of this nation. We are set apart, and serve a different sovereign. Our loyalty is both unassailable and directed away from the state. We own no king but Christ. He is ours, as we are His.

In short, we are deliberate. We are immune, or at least ought to be, from the herd mentality, whether that herd is worshipping some phony civic god or is working itself into a frenzy. We, being people of the Word, are people of thought. Our response is not knee-jerk, but thoughtful. We do not rush out and wallpaper our homes in red, white and blue. We do not look at the smoldering ruins of the World Trade Center and ask, "Why?" but rather look at the whole of the city, our own towns, even our own homes, and ask, "Why not?" And then, again we proclaim the answer—because of the mercy of God.

We will not be diverted. We will not be disrupted. We will not be dissuaded. We will, by the grace of God, continue to be about our calling of building the kingdom of God. And we will do it all for the glory of God alone.

Roughly about the time of the end of the cold war, the culture war became news. Evangelical sociologist J.D. Hunter wrote *Culture Wars*, which became a bestseller. In its wake came Hunter's sequel, *Before The Shooting Begins.* Neo-evangelical Tom Sines fired back with *Cease Fire.* We Reformed folk got involved when my friend Michael Horton tried to rise above the fray with his *Beyond Culture Wars.* Then we signed a deal with the Russians in *Evangelicals and Catholics Together*, and Peter Kreeft invited everyone but the atheists to join the allies in his *Ecumenical Jihad.*

Soon David Wells rode in like some sort of General Douglas MacArthur and weighed in with three separate volumes, and before long not a few scholars and theologians were left scratching their amillennial heads, wondering Whatever Happened to Theology? Suddenly cultural critics disappeared from the radar screen. We need them back.

The bifurcation of the culture wars from the theological wars is a sign of failure on the theological battlefield. Rightly understood, fighting the assumptions and the institutions of the world is what in theology we call fighting *worldliness*. But we don't want to call it that, fearing that the world might begin to call us fundamentalists rather than—when they can suppress their snickering—scholars. We are only willing to fight worldliness if we can fight it on the world's terms.

Culture, we must remember, is religion externalized. It is the justification of our justification, as James argues. It is how we show what it is we believe. Professions of faith are meaningless when we embrace a culture that denies the faith.

That is why we too fight the culture wars, but fight them theologically. J.D. Hunter argued that the antagonists in the battle were the progressives and the orthodox. Orthodox was defined rather loosely, as anyone who affirmed an objective, external, transcendent source of the good and the true. They do not need to agree on what that standard is to join this army, merely that there is a standard. On the other side are the progressives who deny any transcendent source but bicker each other over whose immanent source should prevail.

To fight along these lines, however, is to deny the true transcendent source. If we are at ease with Muslims or Mormons or Roman Catholics as our brothers in battle, we are fighting for something other than the crown rights of King Jesus. And when we do that, we demonstrate to the watching world where our loyalty is.

It was during World War II that C. S. Lewis took pen to paper to defend the reading and studying of great literature. It was argued then that with such a titanic struggle going on, we simply did not have time for such poppycock. Reading Shakespeare was all well and good when things are going fine, but didn't he know there was a war on? Mr. Lewis defended Shakespeare not on the grounds that reading Shakespeare was good for the war effort, nor on the grounds that a war-torn people needed a diversion. Rather he argued that we can not escape culture. There is no culture-less choice; the only question is whether we will invest in good culture or bad culture. Better it should be good culture.

When some of our amillennial brothers suggest that culture is beside the point, that what we need is more dusty tomes on the roots of the Marian controversy in the 17th century, they are not only making the same mistake but are showing themselves to be prisoners of an earlier culture war. They have been overrun by gnosticism and haven't looked up from their scrolls enough to notice. While theology lies beneath the culture wars, there is nothing beyond them. The Lordship of Christ is over all things, and so our calling is to make that manifest in all places.

On the other hand, when others become collaborators by suggesting that we lay down our theological weapons and join forces with Rome, or Salt Lake City, or Constantinople, or Mecca, we must resist that call. No matter how loose the alliance, no matter how wise our strategy, we can rest assured that a pluralistic theology will birth a pluralistic culture. What we believe about Jesus, and the gospel of His kingdom will shape the culture that we build. If we believe that what we believe about Him is a matter of little importance, we build a culture upon sand.

In short, we fight the war on both fronts because we understand that there is but one front. We fight the culture war because the culture is fighting us. It is seeking to shape our theology, just as we hope to see our theology shape it. We must defend ourselves, remembering that while the devil cannot win, he can fight.

Before we can take over culture, in short, we must first free the homeland. We will not succeed until we expel the enemy from our midst. This is the greatest battle of the culture war—to get not culture, but *their* culture, out of our heads and out of our hands, not so that we can go back to our dusty books but so that we can raise up the culture of Him who was raised up.

The culture is not merely the setting of our theological battles but the very prize of the battle. And the theology is not merely the style of our uniform but the very weapon of the battle. We are now, as always, about the compelling business of making visible the invisible kingdom of Jesus Christ. We are bringing all things—not just politics, and not just theology, but all things—under subjection.

Now is not the time to don the blue helmets of the one world worldview. We do not set Jesus aside to go and kill Mohammed. Now is the time—because it is always the time—to grind the head of the serpent into the dust he must eat, in every part of our lives.

Benjamin Franklin said, "Those who are willing to trade civil liberties for temporary security, deserve neither." In the wake of the attacks September 11 this warning looms larger still.

Like everyone else, I was nauseated as I watched the planes hitting the World Trade Center, and then watched the World Trade Center crumble. Like everyone else, my nausea soon turned to resolve: the government must bring the men behind this atrocity to justice.

Often I have argued that the state has been given a ministry by God, but that it has, as with so many states before it, forsaken that ministry to take up others. I have written about state intrusions into the care of the poor, into the business of education, into making sure we eat our vegetables and buckle our seat belts, into the economy as they tinker with their silly paper money.

I have argued that this is a double curse. First, when the state interferes where it should not, it creates havoc. Second, when they enter the battle on the wrong front, they are not in position to wage the war on the proper front. When they are busy handing out cheese their hands are too full to wield the sword.

My hope is that some of this will change now. A frightened nation looks to Washington to pick up that sword, and cheers the soldiers on. With its hands full, perhaps Washington will stay out of our economic and personal lives for a time; there's nothing like an emergency to get one's eyes off distractions.

My fear, however, is more likely to come to pass. There are

those in Washington who would love nothing more than to see us citizens exchange a bit of liberty for greater security. Opinion polls are showing that citizens are now willing to make the exchange, as the great majority of respondents claim they would rather have more wire tapping, computer eavesdropping, etc., if it would help the state to do its job. The trouble is that when the threat abates, the state will not snap back to its original size. Powers gained by the state remain with the state.

Franklin Sanders argues in his novel *Heiland* that states are well aware of this propensity among its citizens. He suggests that a state will intentionally present to the people a great threat so that the people will in turn beg the state to make the threat go away, whatever it takes. I'm not suggesting that the attacks of September 11 were a government plot; I am suggesting that there are those in power now who want nothing more than to make hay while the sun is shining.

But there is a second great fear. States in times of war not only grow more intrusive regarding our privacy, but also regarding the economy. Governments seize whole industries for the sake of the war. They impose wage and price controls. They prop up ailing industries. They ration. And such has already begun.

If anyone wants the airline industry to thrive, it is me; I spend too much time and too much money flying to want to see any of the competitors in this field go under. I also sympathize with their plight. Without the events of September 11, no doubt many of the airlines would have been fine; with them, many are on the brink of destruction. But that does not make it wise, or legal for the federal government to start writing checks to them.

First, it punishes those in the industry who had acted with greater prudence. Remember the ant and the grasshopper. Why should the government tax Southwest Airlines, which, in running a tight ship for years, had accumulated sufficient cash reserves to weather times of hardship, in order to bail out United Airlines which entered September 11 with a week of cash reserves? This only discourages wise preparation. Rewarding a lack of preparation and punishing careful preparation only leads to a greater lack of preparation. That which you subsidize you get more of. Had the weak competitors been allowed to fail, the stronger would have filled those markets with greater efficiency, and we would have all been better off.

Second, it is illegal. Nothing in the Constitution grants the federal government the power to write checks to struggling companies. Such is not among its enumerated powers. The tenth amendment forbids the feds from doing anything that is not among its enumerated powers. The shocking thing is not that they wanted to do this, but that with all our flag waving, no one bothered to check the highest law of the land of the free and the home of the brave to see if what we were applauding was legal. They are lawbreakers, and we cheer them on in ignorance.

But we can afford to practice economic folly. Economic growth is just around the corner, because we are at war. Everyone knows, from the guy who sweeps the halls at CNN, to the high powered economic advisors who serve as their talking heads, that war is good for the economy. Stuff breaks, and having to replace the broken stuff stimulates the economy. Which is why I propose the following. After we have bin Laden's head on a platter, and after Hussein has been sent back to the Stone Age, let's do this. Let's build our war plants right on the beach, and as every tank, every airplane, every bazooka rolls off the line, we'll just dump them in the ocean. Then we'll all be rich.

Friends, you do not get rich by failing to produce. You do not get rich by destroying things. You do not get rich by producing things designed to destroy things. That we have a nation that believes this foolishness is evidence that we are a nation of fools.

Time will tell what God has in store for us. We, citizens of His kingdom, can go forward with confidence, whether the state does well in waging war, or whether Leviathan merely grows larger still. For Leviathan is a tame beast, hanging on the leash of the true King. He is our refuge and our strength. Be at peace, as Leviathan wages war.

Earlier I suggested that the war which the federal government is waging against Afghanistan is a just war. By every standard with which I am familiar, they are in the right. The fighting is not only justifiable, but necessary; not only allowable, but required. Of course the war is unconstitutional, since there has been no declaration of war by the Congress; but since every war we have waged since World War II fits into that category, I won't here make so much of a fuss.

The war is justified because the Afghan government, assuming the reports are true, is complicit in the acts of war/terrorism perpetrated against these United States on September 11. That they have harbored terrorists makes their government guilty. (Their citizens, however, like our victims, are non-combatants, and should be spared all but unintended collateral damage. Toward the Taliban I am a hawk, but I am deeply grieved at those who want to fight terror with terror by bombing citizens indiscriminately. Such is never just war.)

The Taliban has done wrong, and they ought to have a terror for the sword God has given our federal government; the terrorists themselves likewise ought to come under the sword of the United States government. And as I noted, the reports so far all fit these criteria. We have much to be thankful for in the aftermath of this great act of wickedness. We yet have much to labor and pray for, that justice would be done.

Despite all this, however, you will not see me waving the Stars and Stripes, nor is my chest filled with pride over our government. There is no flag on my mailbox, no sticker on my truck, no pin on my jacket. The tsunami of patriotism that is sweeping our land in fact baffles and disturbs me; it strikes me as not just mass hysteria, but mass schizophrenia.

On September 11, 2001, terrorists killed four thousand innocent people. These people did no harm to any Muslim; they didn't even know what a Muslim was. They were not supporters of Israel; they couldn't even locate Israel on a map. The victims were as innocent as one born of man can be. The terrorists were and are harbored by the state in which they live. Many of them even received their terrorist training at the hands of that state. The full force of the government is at the terrorists' disposal for their protection.

These same terrorists, on September 10, killed four thousand more innocents. They have done the same thing every day since September 11, and have been doing so every day since January 22, 1973. The flag that so many of my brothers and sisters are waving so proudly represents the state that harbors these terrorists. I can't fathom how we can be screaming for the blood of the Taliban while honoring a state that licenses its terrorists and calls them medical doctors.

Please do not misunderstand. I'm not suggesting that the abortion terror in our nation justifies the attack of the suicide bombers. I'm not suggesting we should stop pounding the Taliban. I'm not suggesting that we should take it upon ourselves as citizens to attack Washington. I am saying I don't understand all the patriotism, especially within Christ's church and among His people. If we are to vilify those states that harbor terrorists—and we are—why do we not vilify our own state? If we were to measure our love for a given nation by the body count of those ruthlessly butchered by those under the protection of the state, which country ought we to love the least? And yet this is the country we celebrate, to which we pledge our allegiance.

By all means cheer for the brave men in uniform in New York City; by all means celebrate their sacrifice and their heroism. Pray for the safety and the efficacy of the soldiers who have put themselves in harm's way, in order to execute justice. But where are the all-star concerts for the heroes who have been rescuing those doomed to die for years now? Where are the prayers for the soldiers who have fought our own evil for decades?

My friend Steve Baker, and those who work with him, every day sit face to face with those who would be accomplices to terror, mothers planning to hire assassins to kill their babies—and they seek through the power of the gospel to persuade those mothers to choose life. Day by day Steve lives a life of sacrifice through his work at the Bristol crisis pregnancy center.

My friends Jonathan Williams and James Watson and those who work with them likewise give of their time, their wisdom, and their resources to rescue those unjustly sentenced to death, through their work with Bethany Christian Services. Howard Phillips takes to the road and makes a spectacle of himself, running an impossible—though of course, through Christ all things are possible—third party campaign to become our next president, in large part to save future victims of this open terrorism.

Where are the prayers for these brave soldiers? What have we done to honor them? And where are the calls for justice? Why have we not called for the state to use its sword against those who use medicine to kill? Why are we not calling for the state to spill the blood of the blood-stained abortionists?

Meanwhile all the evangelicals are back in their churches saluting the flag of the state that gives sanctuary to terrorists. I refuse to apologize for my refusal to join in the great orgy of patriotism. Instead I not only defend the right, but I proclaim the duty of every Christian to stop this insanity.

If you will not pull the flags down, at least fly them at half staff, for the conscience of the church has died.

ABOUT THE AUTHOR

Dr. R. C. Sproul Jr. is a graduate of Grove City College, Reformed Theological Seminary and Whitefield Theological Seminary. He is also associate pastor of Saint Peter Presbyterian Church and the director of the Highlands Study Center. Dr. Sproul edits *Tabletalk* magazine for Ligonier Ministries, for whom he serves as the Director of Publications. He has written several books, including *Almighty Over All, Dollar Signs of the Times* and *Tearing Down Strongholds*, and he has edited or contributed to several others. Dr. Sproul, his wife Denise, and his five (for now) children—Darby, Campbell, Shannon, Delaney, and Erin Claire—make their home in Meadowview, Virginia.

ABOUT THE
HIGHLANDS STUDY CENTER

The Highlands Study Center exists to help Christians live more simple, separate, and deliberate lives to the glory of God and for the building of His kingdom. As a ministry of Saint Peter Presbyterian Church, we stand with the Westminster Standards. Our hope is to help Reformed believers apply those principles to the way we live our lives. To that end we have a number of ministries, including a resident student program, a college ministry, a community Bible study, and our bi-monthly newsletter *Every Thought Captive*; we also teach classes for homeschoolers, conduct conferences and seminars, and hold an annual Summer Camp for Couples. Please spend some time visiting our website at:

www.highlandsstudycenter.org

ABOUT DRAUGHT HORSE PRESS

Draught Horse Press is privileged to produce and sell books, audio recordings and other materials created by the Highlands Study Center. For more information about our offerings, or for a subscription to our newsletter *Every Thought Captive*, or just to find out more about the work of the Highlands Study Center, please contact us at:

DRAUGHT HORSE PRESS
P.O. Box 1555
Bristol, Tennessee 37621-1555
(877) 244-5184

www.draughthorsepress.com